ORGANIZATION DEVELOPMENT FUNDAMENTALS
Managing Strategic Change

William J. Rothwell, Editor
Cavil S. Anderson
Cynthia M. Corn
Catherine Haynes
Cho Hyun Park
Aileen G. Zaballero

PRESS

ATD Press is an internationally renowned source of insightful and practical information
on workplace learning, training, and professional development.

ATD Press
1640 King Street
Alexandria, VA 22314

Ordering information: Books published by ATD Press can be purchased by visiting ATD's
website at td.org/books or by calling 800.628.2783 or 703.683.8100.

Library of Congress Control Number: 2014952064

ISBN-10: 1-56286-911-6
ISBN-13: 978-1-56286-911-3
e-ISBN: 978-1-60728-502-1

ATD Press Editorial Staff
Director: Kristine Luecker
Manager: Christian Green
Community of Practice Manager, Human Capital: Ann Parker
Associate Editor: Melissa Jones
Cover Design: Marisa Kelly
Text Design: Kristie Carter-George and Marisa Kelly
Printed by Data Reproductions Corporation, Auburn Hills, MI

Contents

Acknowledgments

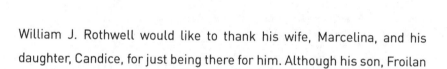

William J. Rothwell would like to thank his wife, Marcelina, and his daughter, Candice, for just being there for him. Although his son, Froilan Perucho, lives in a different state, he is not to be forgotten either.

All the authors of this book would also like to express appreciation to Jong Gyu Park and Aileen Zabellero for their help in coordinating their work.

Preface

Organization development and change management are sometimes terms in search of meaning. They do not have one single definition but instead enjoy a range of meanings—depending on the types of problems to which they are attached.

This book opens with an Advance Organizer to help you focus on the areas in which you have the most to learn. Chapter 1 defines organization development (OD) and change management (CM), and describes the history of each field. Chapter 2 reviews important models that guide the craft of change, including systems theory, Lewin's change model, the critical research model, the action research model, and the appreciative inquiry model.

Chapter 3 switches gears, describing the process of change in OD and examining how to enter change settings, contract with change sponsors, diagnose and assess necessary change, collect data and analyze them, provide feedback about analyzed data to change participants, and plan change efforts. It also describes how to implement change, evaluate change results, institutionalize the change, and separate from the setting.

Chapter 4 reviews the competencies unique to OD change agents, and chapter 5 summarizes important issues in implementing OD change efforts at the individual, group, organization, and international levels. Chapter 6 describes the role played by values and ethics in OD change efforts, while chapter 7 delineates important special issues in OD. Finally, chapter 8 offers some predictions about the future of OD.

Advance Organizer

The Organizer

Complete the Organizer before you read this book. Use it as a diagnostic tool to help you assess what you want to know most about organization development (OD) and change management (CM)—and where you can quickly and easily find it in this book.

Directions

Read each item in the Organizer and circle true (T), not applicable (N/A), or false (F) for each one. Spend about 10 minutes answering the questions. Be honest! Think of organization development and change management as you would like them to be—not what some expert says they are. When you finish, score and interpret the results using the instructions at the end of the Organizer. Share your responses with others in your organization and use them as a starting point for conceptualizing organization development and change management. If you would like to learn more about one of these topics, the number in the far right column corresponds to the book chapter in which the subject is discussed.

The Questions

	Do you believe the organization development or change management in this organization is already:	See chapter:
T N/A F	Aligned with the historical context of OD and/or CM?	1
T N/A F	Attuned to well-regarded definitions of OD and/or CM?	1
T N/A F	Based on a well-known model to guide change?	2
T N/A F	Taking into account approaches for the consultant or facilitator to enter the setting?	3
T N/A F	Taking into account approaches for systematically diagnosing the need for change?	3
T N/A F	Based on effective ways to collect data?	3
T N/A F	Based on effective ways to analyze data?	3
T N/A F	Based on effective ways to feed data back?	3
T N/A F	Based on proven methods to implement change?	3
T N/A F	Based on effective ways to evaluate the change?	3
T N/A F	Based on effective ways to ensure institutionalization of the change?	3
T N/A F	Enacted in accordance with effective OD and CM competencies?	4

T N/A F	Enacted in accordance with effective principles based on the number of people affected by the change?		5
T N/A F	Undertaken in ways consistent with the organization's values?		6
T N/A F	Undertaken in ways consistent with good ethics?		6
T N/A F	Undertaken in ways that considered the application of special issues in OD, such as whole systems?		7
T N/A F	Undertaken in ways that considered future trends in OD?		8
____	Total		

Scoring and Interpreting the Organizer

Give yourself 1 point for each "T" and 0 points for each "F" and "N/A."

Total your score and interpret it as follows:

- **More than 15 points:** Your organization may already have an effective OD or CM program. While improvements can be made, your organization has already mastered many best practice OD or CM principles.

- **13 to 15 points:** Improvements could be made in your organization's OD or CM practices. On the whole, however, your organization is already on the right track.

- **11 to 12 points:** Your organization's OD or CM perceptions are not good. Read this book and plan to make significant improvements.

- **Less than 11 points:** Your organization is far away from effective OD or CM.

1
Introduction
William J. Rothwell

"Change is the only constant."
—Heraclitus, Greek philosopher

This chapter introduces the concepts of organization development and change management. Further, it:

- defines the terms change management (CM) and organization development (OD)
- explains why CM and OD are important
- describes the history of OD and CM.

Defining Change Management

Change management can have many different possible meanings. For some people it means managing expectations about change. For other people it refers to managing communication during an organizational change process. But in common use, change management usually has three distinctive meanings.

Meaning 1: Change Management as a Marketing Term

When the leaders of large consulting firms decided to sell consulting services associated with organizational change, they searched for a "marketing-friendly" term they could use to describe their services. Some sales wizards lighted on the term change management as a phrase that had more market traction than organization development or other such terms. So, in this sense, change management is just an empty marketing phrase.

Meaning 2: Change Management as an Umbrella Encompassing All Ways to Change People

Approximately five approaches other than OD may be used to bring about change in organizations. It is worthwhile considering them.

The first approach is coercion. It is popular with autocratic managers. One way to bring about change is to order people to make a change. Coercion is a management practice associated with punishment. If people are ordered to change and they do not do so, then they may be disciplined, demoted, or fired. (Of course, coercion can also be much more subtle. It can be an implicit threat that an undesirable result will fall to those who fail to go along.)

Coercion has the advantage of being fast. It is easy to order people to act and punish them if they do not make the changes mandated by a manager or executive. But coercion has the disadvantage of not being easily accepted by workers. People often do not like to make changes when they are forced to do so. Coercive managers find that people will resign and go to other companies where they are not threatened with punishment. The price of using coercive management, then, is usually higher turnover.

Another disadvantage is that sometimes workers will sabotage a change when they are threatened with punishment. For example, workers may steal company products or money, or discourage customers

from buying company products or services, as a sub
back at coercive, authoritarian managers.

Coercion is appropriate in times of emergency. When a ship is sink-
ing, a ship's captain is well-advised to order the crew to abandon ship.
The captain will probably not want to take a vote to determine whether the crew wants to abandon ship. In rare cases, such as a company
going into bankruptcy, coercion may be the most appropriate approach
to change.

A second approach to change is persuasion, because one way
to bring about change is to sell people on its benefits. Persuasion is
a management practice associated with rewards—it is the "carrot,"
while coercion is the "stick." If people are sold on making a change and
rewarded for doing it through higher salaries or promotions, then they
have a personal stake in success.

Persuasion has the advantage of appealing to self-interest. People
change because they see a personal benefit to doing so, and they support
the change for that selfish reason. But persuasion has the disadvantage
of being an unsure strategy. Sometimes people do not believe they will
receive the promised benefits from a change. This is particularly true
when the trust level in an organization is low because of a management
team that has the habit of telling half-truths. If that is the history, people
will not be easily "sold" on making the change. Another disadvantage of
persuasion is that it is expensive, because people may have to receive
pay raises or other costly benefits.

Persuasion is appropriate when the manager has access to the
resources needed to make and keep promises. But when the resources
are not sure, another approach to change should be selected, because
there is nothing worse than promising financial benefits that cannot be
given later. Doing that destroys trust and usually angers workers.

A third approach to bringing about change is to use laws or organizational policy. Change the laws or policies and people should change, so the reasoning goes. Governments make laws to prohibit some behaviors and encourage others. Taxation policy, for instance, encourages businesses to do some things—and not do others. The company equivalent of a law is a policy that regulates operations. If the policy is violated, the worker is punished or even fired.

In reality, law and policy are quite similar. They use a legalistic approach to change that forces compliance through a form of coercion. These tactics are appropriate when people cannot be trusted to act for their own benefit or for the benefit of others.

Law and policy have the disadvantage of discouraging behavior. They should not be used when conditions change quickly—or when coercion will actually encourage people to defy authority. In the 1920s, for instance, when alcohol was outlawed in the United States, one unintended result was that people were actually encouraged to drink alcohol more rather than less. Sometimes making something forbidden only increases its appeal. The prohibition law was eventually repealed because it did not achieve its intended result.

A fourth approach to change is leadership change. People have great faith in leaders and heroes. Sometimes they believe that one great person can achieve results even when groups of people fail. One way to bring about change is to change the leaders. Nations do that, on occasion, through nonviolent elections or violent revolutions. In companies, if the board of directors loses confidence in the ability of the chief executive officer (CEO) to achieve results, they will fire him and get someone new. In the same way, if a manager is failing, executives sometimes think that another manager may change the situation. So, they make a leadership change by appointing a new manager.

Leadership change has the advantage of signaling a change to many people. Leadership changes are highly visible and sometimes demonstrate a "sea change." People change because they want the new leader to reward them and not punish them. But leadership change, like persuasion, also has the disadvantage of being an unsure strategy—sometimes leaders cannot change the situation. For instance, a company selling a product that customers do not like will not realize better performance if a new CEO is appointed. The reason, of course, is that the problem has nothing to do with the leader, but rather with the product sold.

Leadership change is appropriate when the old leaders or managers cannot change what they believe and refuse to adopt different strategies when conditions change. But it is an inappropriate strategy if the problems are caused by variables that are not under the control of the leader.

A fifth approach is sometimes called the dialectic approach or the debate approach. An uncommon approach to change is to debate the formal advantages and disadvantages. This approach has actually been used in companies that are considering major strategic changes—such as the purchase of a new company or the sale of an old company.

The approach works just like it does in formal college debates. Two teams are chosen—one team in favor, the other opposed. The two groups rely on formal rules of debates—such as set periods for opening arguments, free argumentation, and closing arguments. The audience, consisting of company senior managers and executives, is asked to keep open minds and even to ask questions. By the end, all the advantages and disadvantages of a proposed change should have been thoroughly explored so that a decision can be reached.

The debate approach has the advantage of getting the facts out quickly and efficiently, assuming both teams prepare. People change because they have had a chance to hear both sides of a carefully planned argument. The idea of using debates and the heat of conflict to find truth is well-known in the legal system. During a court case, two opposing sides—the prosecution and the defense—argue out their positions. The judge is the referee for issues involving law. The jury ultimately decides the facts. But the debate approach has the disadvantage of being only as good as the teams that carry out the debate. If one team forgets import-ant facts, then the debate is not a good one.

The debate approach is appropriate when there are two clear-cut sides to a decision. Unfortunately, organizational decisions are rarely that simple.

Meaning 3: Change Management as Top-Down Change

A third and final way to define change management is to associate it with top-down change, which is different from organization development's unique bottom-up approach.

Think of it like this. Is an organization more like a computer or a growing plant? If you see an organization as more like a computer, then you can believe that groups of people may be programmed much as a computer is programmed. Change can be installed in a linear, step-by-step approach.

Top-down change is sometimes associated with so-called social engineering. While connoting manipulation, social engineering can be more value-neutral than may be implied by the negative idea of manip-ulation, because in that sense it really means applying principles known about people to change them. Human beings, in groups, are akin to herds of animals. Groups can thus be changed by taking advantage of what is known about human behavior in groups.

It should be stressed that top-down change does not mean having leaders tell people what to do; rather, it means uncovering, through research, what success factors are shared in common with effective change efforts and then applying the results of that research across all kinds of change efforts, regardless of what they are. This approach is inherently mechanistic and thus akin to treating organizational change much as a computer programmer manages a computer.

Much research has been done on how to manage change. Harvard theorist John Kotter has studied hundreds of case studies of effective change efforts and isolated common characteristics. In his 1995 book, *Leading Change*, he summarized his model by describing the eight common steps shared by effective change efforts:

1. Build a sense of urgency: Excite the head and heart of all people in the organization so they see the need for change.

2. Enlist a group of powerful supporters: Get a group of people who will support the change and will help to drive it.

3. Clarify the vision of what success will look like: Help people to see what success will look like once a dream of the future is realized.

4. Communicate the vision: Sell others on the vision.

5. Eliminate obstacles to change: Identify what gets in the way of success and get rid of any obstacles.

6. Build enthusiasm by creating short-term wins: Show people that success can be achieved by demonstrating quick wins that will energize people to see that success can be attained.

7. Ensure that the change lasts: Aim for sustainability of change.

8. Make the change part of the corporate culture: Build the change into the normal daily activities of the organization.

Many such top-down models have been published. Most are based on research about change practices that work in organizational settings.

Another approach is to study why change fails and then guide decision-makers during a change effort to avoid those common mistakes. About 60 to 70 percent of all change efforts fail. Common reasons include:

- A change effort has unexpected consequences. Example: an organization implements a "smoking cessation policy." While a desirable policy on its face, care must be taken to avoid unintended consequences—such as loss of productivity as smokers take lengthy off-the-premises breaks to smoke.

- A change effort is not supported by all key stakeholders. Some decision-makers supported the change, but others did not. Those who did not eventually destroyed the change effort.

- The needs that prompted interest in change can evolve over time, causing leaders to lose interest. Example: An organization launches a succession planning effort and it appears to work in preparing people for promotion. When decision-makers see that a problem is being solved, they lose interest and therefore support for the change itself wanes.

In change management, managers are given a change model to follow. They apply it whenever they are tasked to make a change effort. It does not matter what the change effort is: The same model is used for anything.

An important advantage of the top-down approach is that it is predictable. Once employees and managers alike know what the steps in the model are, they know what will follow when the first step is taken. That leads to greater predictability in the change process, which can reduce the resistance to change if change participants face the unexpected.

An important disadvantage of the top-down approach is that it loses flexibility. Managers and workers must follow the same steps regardless of the change process. Doing so reduces the ability to modify change to accommodate unique challenges faced in any change effort.

Defining Organization Development

OD is usually known to mean bottom-up change. It is a long-term change effort focused on improving the interpersonal relationships of employees. OD usually involves internal or external consultants to facilitate the change process. These consultants apply the practical aspects of psychology, sociology, anthropology, and political science to organizational challenges.

Bottom-up change does not mean that workers make decisions and managers follow them; rather, it means that the change process itself is changed as necessary to accommodate people, problems, situations, external competitive conditions, and other factors that may influence the way change is designed, implemented, evaluated, and communicated. Its goal is to involve people in the change process because an important assumption of OD is that change is more likely to be accepted if all those affected by a change have a say in making decisions that shape the direction of the change. Given the flexibility with which the change process itself is approached, OD practitioners usually regard it as an organic process, akin to the way a plant grows.

One important influence on OD is so-called *person-centered psychology*, a view of psychology that regards the psychologist as "holding up a mirror" to clients to help them see themselves better. Unlike the doctor-patient view of medicine in which doctors regard themselves as experts whose role is to diagnose a problem to its root causes, person-centered psychologists believe that the best experts are the clients themselves because they already know what their problems are, what their solutions should be, and what results they seek.

The History of Change Management and Organization Development

The roots of change management and organization development have probably existed since the dawn of prehistory. It is easy to imagine that early rulers expected to issue an order and simply have it carried out—often on pain of death for those who did not meet their expectations. In early history, change was assumed to be easy because the world did not change much. People were simply expected to follow their leaders. And when leaders sometimes became too aggressive or were proven to be unreasonable, they were overthrown and new leaders took over.

Modern thinking about change management dates from the dawn of the Industrial Revolution, when technology was first introduced to the production process. Workers, who were primarily doing manual labor, were poorly educated. They were aided by tools and other equipment to achieve results. In that context, business owners were like monarchs, managers and supervisors were like aristocrats, and workers were like peasants who toiled under close direction. Organizations were perceived as machines. Change was managed in an arbitrary, ad hoc manner.

But as the Industrial Revolution progressed the work became more sophisticated. Machinery and technology became more complex, which meant the workers who toiled on those machines and with that technology had to become more skilled and knowledgeable.

Beginning with the Hawthorne studies in the 1920s, researchers became aware that the way human beings were treated in work settings could affect productivity. Simply paying attention to people had a greater impact on their productivity than variations in external environmental factors, such as lighting. People, previously an ignored resource, began to attract attention as critical to the production process.

Seminal thinkers of the 1930s and 1940s laid the foundation for modern thinking about change management and organization development. Kurt Lewin (1898-1947) pinpointed *group dynamics* to explain the phenomenon of people working together to achieve results. He noted that action research could be foundational in change efforts and, as early as World War II, experimented with ways to consult collaboratively with groups to achieve improved results. The term organization development was first used in the 1950s by Douglas McGregor and Richard Beckhard to describe their approach to consulting, which did not match older, expert-driven approaches to diagnosing organizational problems in a quest for solutions. At about the same time, the first efforts were being made to use laboratory training in which participants in off-the-job settings focused on their interpersonal interaction (group process or group dynamics), rather than on training content. When the participants were unable to transfer what they had learned back to their jobs, experimenters followed them back to their work sites. This led to the first *T-Groups* (standing for "training groups") in which people focused their attention on interpersonal relationships and ways of working together in work settings.

Around 1945, Rensis Likert began using surveys as a foundation for change in organizational settings. Building on the work of Kurt Lewin, Likert found that surveys could be used to pinpoint organizational problems more directly than filtering information through managers and executives. His unique approach, called survey-guided development, used surveys to uncover what people perceived to be their problems and then feed that back to managers and workers as a basis for improvement.

First-generation contributors to OD thus included seminal names like Kurt Lewin and Rensis Likert. When the OD field first came into its own as a recognizable field of research and practice, a second generation of contributors was born, including Warren Bennis, Edgar Schein, and Richard Beckhard. The third generation of contributors to OD included such names as Warner Burke, Larry Greiner, Edward Lawler III, Newton Margulies, and Anthony Raia. Fourth-generation contributors include Dave Brown, Thomas Cummings, Max Elden, and Jerry Porras.

As discussed at length in the last chapter of this book, the future of OD and the direction of the field is uncertain. However, it seems likely that growing interest will continue to evolve around making OD more positive (appreciative inquiry), comprehensive and systematic (whole systems transformational change), and related to how humans and technology can effectively work together to achieve results (sociotechnical systems).

2
Organization Development and Change Models

Cavil S. Anderson and
Aileen G. Zaballero

*"A model for change is a simplified representation of the general steps
in initiating and carrying out a change process. It is rooted in solid
research and theory."*
—**Rothwell and Sullivan 2005, 39**

This chapter reviews five key organization development and change management models, focusing on key features, benefits, and limitations. An OD manager's tool is also included. The chapter also discusses:

- why organization development and change management models are important
- what an organizational diagnosis does
- the fundamentals of systems theory.

The Importance of Models

Models can illustrate and help assess organizational change. They act as guides for consultants, serving as road maps about what to do and how to do it. More importantly, models can clarify how to optimize change efforts. Organizational models enable users to become familiar with, and draw conclusions about, what to observe in an organization. Burke (Howard and Associates 1994) formulated and explained how organizational models are valuable, stating that models:

- increase knowledge of organizational behavior
- help to classify organizational data
- help users interpret data about an organization
- promote understanding and explanations of what the users observe.

Furthermore, organizational models provide a systematic approach to collect data, identify vital information to analyze, and illustrate the nature of the relationships between key variables. Without models to guide the process, practitioners may be inclined to collect and analyze data based on guesswork or management caprice. Organizational diagnosticians, like medical physicians, collect and evaluate organizational data to design an appropriate intervention. Although many diagnosticians use conceptual models intuitively, it is important to contemplate the complexity of organizations and the enormous amount of data available for analysis. That is particularly true in this age of big data, which are sometimes collected without big analysis.

In addition, practitioners must consider the unique needs of their organizations and the dynamics of the individuals involved. Selecting the model with the best fit for the organization can make a significant difference between an efficient/effortless change and an inept/challenging change effort. Therefore, understanding the driving and restricting forces of a change requires thoughtful consideration of how change impacts individuals and the social components of organizations (Kezar 2001). A starting point for change leaders is to conduct an organizational diagnosis that examines the internal and external issues affecting an organizational change effort.

What Is an Organizational Diagnosis?

At the beginning of any change effort, there is a need to know why change is required. Diagnosis, whether conducted by consultants, managers, workers, or some combination, is an important starting point in change management and organization development, although the approaches may differ.

"In organizational diagnosis, managers use conceptual models and applied methods to assess an organization's current state and discover ways to solve problems, meet challenges, or enhance performance" (Harrison 2005, 1). With roots in community, management, and leadership development, organization development and change have a rich history. Many OD and change management models exist to guide interventions intended to improve organizational effectiveness and to adapt as conditions continuously change (Beer and Spector 1993; Cummings and Worley 1993; Rothwell and Sredl 1992).

The diagnostic process usually involves assessing the organization's current condition by guiding what to look at—this is also the first step in selecting the appropriate change strategies and interventions. Diagnosis as a concept is similar to how a physician conducts tests and collects a patient's vital information as a means to evaluate the human system (Tichy, Hornstein, and Nisberg 1977). This initial process is a critical step that allows the physician to make informed decisions and prescribe an appropriate course of treatment. It is also similar to the process by which psychologists guide their clients through a process of self-discovery to recognize their own problems/challenges, discover the barriers that prevent improvement, and establish ways to reduce the impact of those barriers. Furthermore, an organizational diagnostician analyzes the organization as a system that interacts with its internal and external environment. The total system includes all information including inputs, throughputs, and outputs, as well as feedback loops linking those inputs, throughputs, and outputs. This perspective represents open systems theory (Katz and Kahn 1978).

In addition, organizations can be examined from at least three levels: organizational, group, and individual. Figure 2-1 is an adaptation of Harrison's Model for Diagnosis of Individual and Group Behavior (2005), which illustrates the importance of considering all variables that impact the organization.

Figure 2-1. Organizational Diagnosis Model

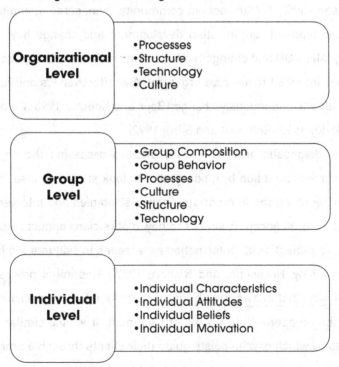

Organizational Level
- Processes
- Structure
- Technology
- Culture

Group Level
- Group Composition
- Group Behavior
- Processes
- Culture
- Structure
- Technology

Individual Level
- Individual Characteristics
- Individual Attitudes
- Individual Beliefs
- Individual Motivation

Adapted from Harrison (2005, 56).

The Fundamentals of Systems Theory

Proposed in the 1940s by the biologist Ludwig von Bertalanffy, and furthered by Ross Ashby, systems theory focuses on the "arrangement of and relations between the parts [and] how they work together as a whole" (Ansari 2004, 1). Von Bertalanffy highlighted that real systems are open and interact with their environments, which require overall continuous evolution to improve, as opposed to improvement through the isolation of its parts or elements (Heylighen and Joslyn 1992).

Systems theory provides a framework for classifying and evaluating change in organizational settings. It is an interdisciplinary study that fuses multiple disciplines into a coherent body of theory and practice. Without a systemic orientation, there is no motivation to look at how the components of a system interrelate. "By enhancing each of the other disciplines, it continually reminds us that the whole can exceed the sum of its parts" (Senge as cited in French and Bell 1995, 87).

Systems thinking and systems theory explain how we understand, guide, and approach change in organizations. In a nutshell, a system is a structured set of collections of parts, or subsystems, that interact together to achieve an overall goal or objective. The *input* is something that goes into a system—transformational processes add value to the inputs by acting upon them—and the *output* is the system's product or outcome. For example, when building a computer (a transformational process), the inputs will include all the necessary resources—such as people, machinery, and raw materials—that are essential to achieving outputs or results: a finished computer. Together, the inputs, transformational processes, and outputs produce the desired result. One key thing to consider in systems theory is the interconnection of all the parts. In other words, if a small change is made to one variable of the system, it can potentially make a dramatic change to other variables and inevitably to the entire system. It is essential to fully understand the relationship between all variables and how change can potentially impact every component of the system.

It is easy to think of an example. Picture a spider web. Tug one strand of the web and the entire web vibrates. In systems theory the same principle applies: Make one change to one part of the system and all other parts are affected, sometimes predictably and sometimes not.

There are various types and forms of systems in organizations that range from simple to complex. *Complex systems* are composed of various subsystems. These subsystems can sometimes appear as hierarchical or horizontal, and are amalgamated and integrated to accomplish an overall goal. Each subsystem has its own parameter, which is bound by various inputs, processes, outputs, and outcomes to achieve an overall goal. A complex system is considered a high-functioning system when the various subsystems continuously interact and exchange feedback to ensure that they remain aligned and focused on achieving the overall goal. If any part or activity of the subsystems is misaligned or is not responding, the system's overall function will be impacted. Consider a cup of water: It cannot be seen as a system because, if you remove some of the water, by drinking or pouring it, you still have a cup of water. Now consider a car: If you remove the brakes, wheels, or engine, the overall function of the car is impacted and it will no longer function.

Systems Thinking

Jay Forrester, a professor at MIT, proposed systems thinking in 1956. It differs fundamentally from traditional forms of analysis, which focus on breaking something down into individual pieces. Systems think-ing, in contrast, focuses on the interactions and connections between subsystems within a system. Instead of isolating parts, systems thinking expands to take into account the numbers of interactions. Thus, those who ascribe to systems thinking will reach different findings than those who use traditional forms of analysis. This is especially influential when what is being studied is complex or has a great deal of influence from other sources inside or outside the organization (Aronson 1992).

Many problems that organizations face are complex and involve multiple stakeholders. Often, these challenges are a result of past actions taken to implement change. However, it is important to remember that change is a process, not an isolated event. Change does not occur instantaneously, nor do all people adopt it quickly. The transition from a current state to a future state requires the effective management of a system's human components.

Hence, systems thinking encourages practitioners to shift to a different way of thinking—by seeking out how parts of a large whole are interconnected. Understanding the significance of organizational models, organizational diagnosis, systems theory, and thinking will enable practitioners to guide the change process more effectively.

Organization Development Models

Organization development (OD) is a way to implement change that is participative in nature. In other words, it involves everyone affected by the change. OD efforts focus on changing groups, while concentrating on individual participation. Unlike most change efforts, which are managed from the top down, OD is a grassroots effort that is implemented as a bottom up initiative. In addition, according to Rothwell, Stavros, Sullivan, and Sullivan (2010), the key points of an OD effort are:

- long-range in perspective
- best implemented when supported by top managers

- primarily effecting change through education
- interrelated to organizational learning.

In OD, "the entire system is accountable rather than just management" (Rothwell et al. 2010, 14).

Two major change models used in OD are action research and appreciative inquiry, which will be discussed in the following sections.

Action Research

One foundational model of OD is action research, which is broadly viewed as a process, model, theory, and set of techniques used to address issues and problems.

As a set of techniques, action research guides OD practitioners in the change process, but does not dictate exactly what they should do in any situation. As a process, action research is a cycle that incorporates the eight steps to implementing a change—entering the system or organization, clarifying what is happening, assessing and feeding back issues from the standpoint of participants in the system, facilitating action planning among participants, implementing the change, evaluating the change, ensuring that the change is adopted, and leaving the setting. As a model, action research is a visual representation that illustrates complex activities in a participative change effort. Finally, as a theory, action research is a participatory worldview that aims to bring together action, reflection, and participation to obtain practical solutions (Reason and Bradbury 2001, 1).

This definition incorporates the five key principles of action research:
- Pragmatic: It addresses practical issues and links theory with practice.
- Democratic: It involves people and also seeks to empower them to generate their own knowledge.

- Extended epistemology: It accommodates many ways of knowing, valuing the experiential, narrative, aesthetic, and conceptual.

- Value-oriented: It asks how we can contribute to the economic, political, psychological, and spiritual well-being of humans, communities, and the wider ecology.

- Developmental: It evolves over time toward a more significant diagnostic model (Reason and Bradbury 2001; Reason and McArdle n.d.).

Action research emphasizes involvement and participation by all those affected by a change. Specifically, action research guides people through the systematic examination of a problem and possible solutions to it. The OD practitioner applying action research will implement an ongoing, cyclical process that focuses on refining the methodological tools used and needed in each given situation (O'Brien 1998). In short, OD practitioners seek to guide people through their own problem-solving and solution-finding processes, rather than trying to impose expert opinions, which often creates resistance.

Applying Action Research: A Case Study

An educational institution implemented an action research process to create learning-networks across several departments.

Five different departments within the same college attempted to map out a process to implement strategy to achieve the organization's strategic objectives. A coordinating committee of three people was appointed. Each department began by listing and prioritizing the department's strategic goals for that particular period. After completing this exercise the lists were compared. Findings indicated that very few of the department's strategic priorities were the same. Furthermore, interpretations of the strategic plan and the mission also differed. Two of the five departments had similar directions and perspectives, whereas the views of the other departments were very different.

The coordinating committee acknowledged that each department was coming from a different philosophical viewpoint, driven by departmental specialization. It was determined that, if managed effectively, an action research approach could be effective, because it would allow each department to focus on its own particular needs, while simultaneously focusing on solving the organizational problem. The coordinating committee was able to structure the activities that shaped the intervention based on the feedback from each department.

Using the action research approach allowed the participants to solve long-standing challenges that could not be solved by a quick-fix training effort. It facilitated a revision of the organizational structure into a more flexible design that created a cross-functional, multi-departmental team. Both leadership and management development efforts improved the ability of managers to take charge of their own departmental challenges. In addition, the transfer of learning was increased because employees were allowed to contribute to the solution and take immediate action.

Action research is client centered, problem centered, and action oriented. Figure 2-2 illustrates the steps of the action research process, giving a brief explanation of each phase.

Figure 2-2. Process of Action Research

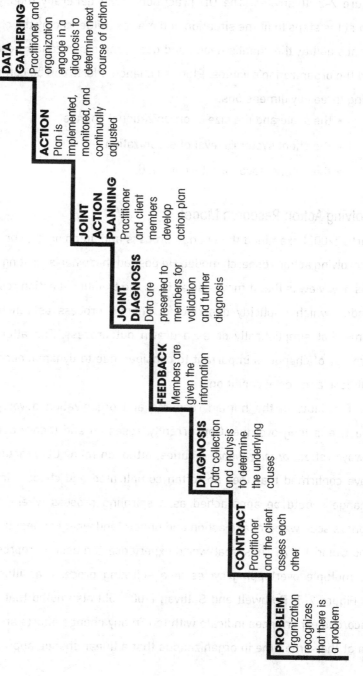

PROBLEM
Organization recognizes that there is a problem

CONTRACT
Practitioner and the client assess each other

DIAGNOSIS
Data collection and analysis to determine the underlying causes

FEEDBACK
Members are given the information

JOINT DIAGNOSIS
Data are presented to members for validation and further diagnosis

JOINT ACTION PLANNING
Practitioner and client members develop action plan

ACTION
Plan is implemented, monitored, and continually adjusted

DATA GATHERING
Practitioner and organization engage in a diagnosis to determine next course of action

Adapted from Schein (1999), Rothwell and Sullivan (2005), and Cummings and Worley (2009).

The different phases in actual practice are not as methodical as Figure 2-2 illustrates. The OD practitioner will generally modify and adjust the steps to fit the situation and may be influenced by the change agent's ability, the client's needs and goals, the organization's context, and the organization's values. Planned change efforts can be compared using three key dimensions:

- the scale and the size of organizational change
- the client system's level of organization
- the setting (local or international).

Evolving Action Research Model

Burke (2002) examined the change process and, in doing so, conceived an evolving action research model. He posited that what is exciting about this new view is that it moves away from the traditional action research model, which implicitly describes a change process as functioning somewhat simplistically or as a drawn out process. The alternative strategy of change is important to consider, due to dynamic economic, political, and social conditions.

Flexibility in the human resource and organization development practice is long overdue. Concurrently, research and theory does not always reflect *organizational* realities, although many OD practitioners have confirmed that they are often complicated and chaotic. Instead, change should be approached as a spiraling process where practitioners seek ways to take action and understand what happened (Weick and Quinn 1999). Thus, real-world experience can best be represented as multiple overlapping cycles in a spiraling process, as illustrated in Figure 2-3. Rothwell and Sullivan (2005, 55) also noted that recent recorded experiences indicate with too "many change efforts are going on at the same time in organizations that a linear change approach no longer works." Too many concurrent change efforts lead to a crowding out effect, as well as burn-out among employees—it is simply not possible to remember everything going on at once.

A new model—one that does not assume a project-oriented beginning, middle, and an end to a change effort—is necessary to guide change. These efforts should be regarded as continuing.

Figure 2-3. Phases of Action Research

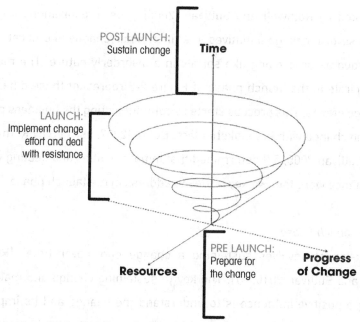

Adapted from Burke (2002), as cited in Rothwell and Sullivan (2005).

Pre-Launch Phase

Figure 2-3 plots the change on a three-dimensional axis, where the y-axis is time, the x-axis is the progress of change, and the z-axis is resources (such as people, money, or technology). The period of time before the change effort begins is referred to as the pre-launch phase.

According to Burke (2002 as cited by Rothwell et al. 2010), this phase encompasses activities that require leaders to:

- Examine the external environment—what is the business case for change?
- Establish the need for change—why must the change happen?
- Provide clarity of the vision and direction of the change—what will a successful change look like?

Launch Phase

As noted by Rothwell and Sullivan (2005), most organizations implement several change initiatives at a time. Since change is cyclical, it is regarded as proceeding like spirals in a disorderly nature. The multiple spirals in the launch phase of Figure 2-3 represent these different change efforts. This process starts by communicating the business case for the change with key stakeholders. Burke (2002, as cited by Rothwell and Sullivan 2005, 57) determined that initial activities and dealing with resistance were the two key issues to address in the launch phase.

Post-Launch Phase

"Post-launch involves sustaining a change effort over time" (Rothwell and Sullivan 2010, 57). The key to sustaining change and maintaining a positive influence is to understand the change and its impact. Every change affects stakeholders at multiple levels and in multiple ways, which is emphasized by incorporating what is learned into subsequent phases.

Appreciative Inquiry

Appreciative inquiry (AI), according to David Cooperrider (2005), is an appraisal of what is the best in people, their organizations, and the world around them. Unlike the action research model, which focuses on solving a problem, AI seeks to leverage what is working well and further develop the positive aspects of the organization and its people. The following questions are typically asked in any AI change effort:

- What gives life to a living system?
- When does the system seem the most alive?
- What makes the system most effective?

At the heart of AI is the way questions are asked, because they serve as catalysts for change. Questions support the organization's ability to capture, foresee, and inspire a positive influence. AI emphasizes strengths, achievements, unexplored potentials, opportunities, values, customs, tactical abilities, lived stories, knowledge, and understandings of the deeper organizational spirit and vision. In addition, AI seeks to build constructive associations among people and operates from a positive change point of view (Cooperrider and Whitney 2005).

Appreciation is acknowledging and valuing the inputs and qualities of people around us. *Inquiry* is the investigation and discovery of better ways of understanding, and being open to new discoveries. By appreciating what is good and valuable in the present situation, people are able to discover and learn about opportunities for positive change.

The traditional approach to change focuses on the problem with the assumption that something is broken and needs to be fixed. Unfortunately, that can provoke a defensive response in which more attention is devoted to finding someone to blame for the problem, rather than finding a worthwhile solution. The alternative is the AI approach, where the focus is on what is going well and being done right in the organization. This approach avoids defensive responses and promotes creativity and innovation.

One of the original AI models is the 4D model, which includes four phases: discover, dream, design, and deliver. An alternative mode is the 4I model, which also consists of four phases: initiate, inquire, imagine, and innovate. Figure 2-4 is an illustration of the 5D model.

Figure 2-4. 5D Method of Appreciative Inquiry

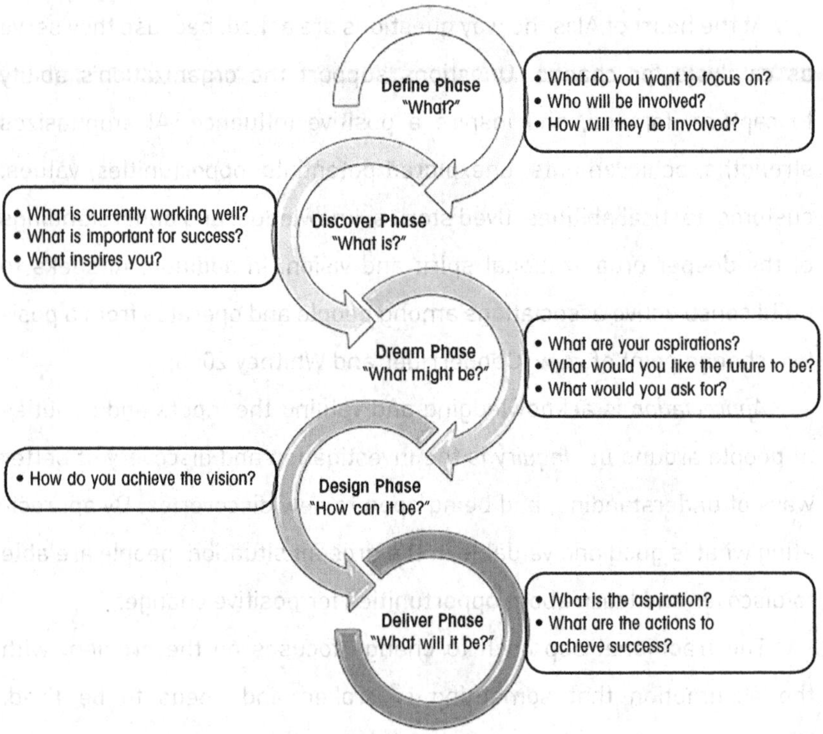

Define Phase "What?"
- What do you want to focus on?
- Who will be involved?
- How will they be involved?

Discover Phase "What is?"
- What is currently working well?
- What is important for success?
- What inspires you?

Dream Phase "What might be?"
- What are your aspirations?
- What would you like the future to be?
- What would you ask for?

Design Phase "How can it be?"
- How do you achieve the vision?

Deliver Phase "What will it be?"
- What is the aspiration?
- What are the actions to achieve success?

Applying Appreciative Inquiry: Case Study

Two shift managers attended a weeklong training program on appreciative inquiry and decided to see if the principles of the approach would make a difference for the employees they managed. These two managers experienced high levels of employee turnover, which made teamwork difficult because they had to spend most of their time recruiting, orienting, and training new employees. By implementing an AI initiative, they hoped to improve the situation.

The managers focused on the team's strengths and tried to build on them. The first step was to isolate and define what they were going to focus on during the change. For example, instead of looking for ways to fix high employee turnover problems, they chose to emphasize ways to retain staff. The change of view had a significant impact on what they were trying to change.

In step two, the discovery phase, the managers searched for what was currently working well for their group. They polled all their employees, using questions that got the group to acknowledge, appreciate, and value what has worked well and to get people talking positively. They also identified the factors that contributed to the organization's past successes, which helped them appreciate and value the best of what has worked.

The managers next identified their team's dreams of what might be in step three, the dream phase. By using the positive strengths identified in the previous phase, the managers were able to support their desires to institutionalizing these strengths. However, if this had not been the case, the managers could have identified a diverse group of employees and tasked them with coming up with a creative or innovative vision of the future.

During the design phase, step four, the managers designed the types of systems, processes, and strategies that would enable the dream to be realized. They also took into account what was necessary to support their vision and who should be involved.

The final stage, the deliver or destiny phase, called for the managers and team members to put their practical strategies into operation and created a place for the team's ideas to emerge and develop. During this phase it is important to make sure that the dream central to the plan occurs and is supported and sustained throughout the organization. The managers focused on encouraging and allowing their employees to take action.

Both action research and appreciative inquiry are change models that rely on the participation of everyone involved. Although the OD process can be more time consuming and costly than manager-driven change, it has the potential for increased sustainability because everyone takes responsibility for the success, rather than just one manager or a consultant.

On the other hand, many organizations seek to implement change faster and in a more controlled manner. The following section will discuss the two commonly used change models: McKinsey 7-S Model and Kotter's Eight-Step Change Model.

Change Management Models

Organizational leaders must decide "how" and "what" to change. In many cases, they know what they want to change but are not clear about how to get there. Knowing how to change is challenging because most organizations fail to identify and demonstrate the need for it. Change management models are important to help address the complexity of change and the unpredictability of human behavior. The following section will discuss two change management models that are widely used: the McKinsey 7-S Model and Kotter's Eight-Step Change Model.

McKinsey 7-S Model

Tom Peters, Robert Waterman, Richard Pascale, and Anthony Athos created the McKinsey 7-S Model (shown in Figure 2-5) while they were working for McKinsey (Waterman, Peters, and Phillips 1980). This strategic model collectively determines how a company will operate and is referred to as a holistic approach. It can be used to:

- Align organizational performance.

- Understand the essential and most significant factors in an organization's strategy.

- Determine how to best realign an organization to a new strategy or other organizational design.

- Analyze the current functions and relations of an organization.

Figure 2-5 shows the McKinsey 7-S Model, which is made up of seven different considerations:

- Shared values represent the mission of the company and are the core value of the model because they symbolize what the organization believes in and stands for.

- Strategy implies how the organization will respond to changes in its external environment.

- Structure refers to the organizational design, such as reporting lines, coordination, and task allocation.

- Systems represent the supporting systems, processes, and procedures, such as information systems, financial and payment systems, and resource allocation.

- Staff represents who is employed, as well as the number and types (and role) of employees.

- Style implies the overarching leadership, management style, and culture of the organization.

- Skills specify the proficiencies, talents, and competencies of the employees in the organization (Waterman, Peters, and Phillips 1980; Recklies 2007).

Figure 2-5. McKinsey 7-S Model

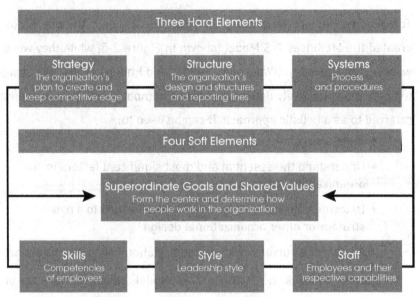

Adapted from Peters and Waterman (1982).

The seven elements can also be divided into hard and soft skills—with the hard skills comprising strategy, structure, and systems, and the soft skills comprising shared values, skills, staff, and style. Furthermore, the foundation of the model is based on the theory that, for an organization to perform well, these seven elements need to be aligned and mutually reinforced. Thus, the model can help identify what needs to be realigned to improve performance or maintain alignment (and performance) during other types of change.

Figure 2-6 provides a brief illustration of the use of the 7-S model to implement a balanced scorecard.

Figure 2-6. Application of McKinsey 7-S Model

7-S Model Elements	Examples of Questions to Ask	Possible Responses
Strategy	• What is our strategy trying to accomplish? • What are the objectives? • What is distinct about the organization? • What makes us competitive? • What other environmental factors should we consider?	• Implement a balance scorecard to measure performance • To measure employee and organization performance • It's a learning organization • Demand for product • Keep ahead of competition
Structure	• How is the organization structured? • What are the reporting relationships? • How are decisions made? • How is information shared?	• Flat and decentralized • Flat and horizontal • Centrally • Daily formal and informal
Systems	• What are the main systems that will drive the implementation? • What controls are in the organization? • How is progress tracked?	• Financial, resource planning and tracking, information management, and communication • A representative committee • Daily and weekly meetings
Staff	• What is the size of the staff? • Are there gaps in required positions? • What types and skills are needed to support the implementation?	• 120 • One in senior management, two middle management, and eight specialist within units • Change agents and team players in every unit to drive learning and ensure implementation

7-S Model Elements	Examples of Questions to Ask	Possible Responses
Style	• What is the leadership style of the organization? • Does the organization have participative team or basically just units and groups of people? • Do employees function collaboratively or competitively?	• Participative and will be the first level to be trained on the balanced scorecard • Unit and cross-functional teams • Collaborative and cooperative
Skills	• What skills are required to deliver and implement the product? • How will the training be monitored?	• Conflict management, problem solving, data analysis, and decision making • Weekly reflection and feedback sessions
Shard Values	• What is the mission of the organization? • What are the organization's values? • Are the mission and values aligned with the strategy? • What is the organizational culture?	• Deliver high quality products • Integrity, honesty, and transparency • Strategy speaks of a learning organization • Encourage and empower employees to improve continuously

The McKinsey S-7 Model also has many benefits and disadvantages. The four key benefits are:

- an effective approach to diagnose and make sense out of the organization

- a way to direct organizational change

- a combination of both rational and emotional elements are considered

- all parts are interconnected, which requires a holistic approach.

The major disadvantage is the interrelated nature of the parts, where if one part changes the entire organization will change. The model also tends to overlook differences in organizational design and complexity (Peters and Waterman 1982).

Kotter's Eight-Step Change Model

John Kotter, a Harvard Business School professor and leading researcher on organizational change management, indicated that 70 percent of all change efforts fail because most organizations do not take a systems and holistic approach to change (Kotter 1995). Kotter's model is both systems-oriented and holistic.

Kotter's Eight-Step Change Model (Figure 2-7) is highly regarded as an effective approach to managing change. It has become very popular and is quite practical. Kotter relates this approach to people's reaction to change—how people see, feel, and then change. Each stage acknowledges and identifies what people should do to change.

Figure 2-7. Kotter's Eight Steps Process for Leading Successful Change

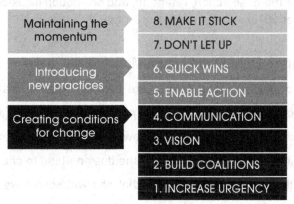

Source: Kotter (1995).

1. Increase urgency: Employees need to see that a change is necessary for the organization to survive. It is critical to communicate that the change can be achieved without any damaging effects (such as retrenchments).

2. Build a cohesive team: Build a team for the change, with respected and appreciated employees within the organization.

3. Hypothesize the vision: The vision needs to articulate a clear path to how the change will improve the future of the organization and workers' jobs.

4. Communicate the vision: For the vision to work it must be completely acknowledged, approved, and accepted by the employees. That means the leaders of the change group must follow by example.

5. Empower: the employees to implement the change. It is also important for management to follow the same guidelines and rules as the employees, leading by example.

6. Create short-term milestones: This allows managers to indicate progress made, which makes it easier for employees to acknowledge and accept change. Incentives to change are also key to this phase.

7. Be persistent: Continuously encourage change to sustain it.

8. Make the change permanent: Institutionalize the change into organizational culture and practices by modifying employee recruitment, selection, retention, and promotion decisions (Kotter 2012).

Applying Kotter's Eight-Step Change Model: Case Study

Cindy is the owner of a local bakery, but has struggled to maintain a steady flow of customers in the past months. The reasons for this change included a poor economy and newly opened grocery store with a bakery within 12 miles of her shop. If she does nothing to change the current conditions, Cindy has realized that she will soon have to look for another job. After much deliberation and consideration, she decided to introduce a variety of whole wheat breads, with a goal of generating additional revenue and maintaining a competitive edge over the other bakery in the area. She knows from experience how important it is to use a change model to guide the process, and decided to apply Kotter's eight-step model. Figure 2-8 summarizes her actions.

Exhibit 2-8. Application of Kotter's Eight-Step Change Model

Kotter's Eight-Step	Cindy's Bakery Action Steps
Step 1: Establish a Sense of Urgency	• Hold a meeting with staff to discuss the current financial situation. • Inform employees that they are on the verge of losing their jobs due to the limited revenue coming in. • Explain the need for change at the bakery and show the connection between making the changes and creating job security. • Employees recognize that their jobs are in jeopardy and express commitment to making whatever changes necessary to avoid layoffs.
Step 2: Create a Guiding Coalition	• Employees understand the sense of urgency for change and decide who the members of the guiding coalition will be. • Choose employees to form the coalition that will help acquire the necessary equipment for bread baking, learn the process of bread baking and train the other employees, market and advertise the extended menu, determine pricing and quantity, and create space in the bakery for new machines and storage. • These employees will provide the necessary direction for developing and implementing the new menus.
Steps 3 and 4: Create and Communicate a Vision for Change	• Provide all employees with a clear vision of what the change is about. • Create a vision that connects the extended menu to the long-term sustainability of the bakery. • Once the vision is written, communicate it to the entire staff. • Communicate to the employees what is in it for them.
Step 5: Empower Broad-Based Action	• Identify and remove potential barriers to efficiency. • Make sure that the employees have all the resources to accomplish the respective tasks. • Make sure the bakery has adequate staff to begin offering this extended menu. • Promote the service to new and existing customers. • Address barriers immediately.

Kotter's Eight-Step	Cindy's Bakery Action Steps
Step 6: Generate Short-Term Wins	• Provide performance expectations and incentives. • Check in with members of the guiding coalition to acknowledge successful efforts to keep them motivated to continue to work toward project goals. • Recognize successful efforts publicly.
Step 7: Produce More Change	• Focus on the role of early success as an enabler of future success—for example, hold a staff appreciation event that could also focus on team building at the same time. • Provide a platform for the recognition of those involved in the project and their achievements. • Demonstrate future milestones and reinforce the vision.
Step 8: Anchor the Changes	• Monitor acceptance of extended items and how well the organizational culture is adapting to having them on the menu. • Encourage employees to explore new services independently and report back on ideas that might lead to adding items to the menu. • This will better prepare employees to be ready for new services that might be introduced in the future.
Key Point: Kotter's model can be universally applied to a variety of change situations to promote the successful implementation of change in any organization.	

The two advantages of this model are that it is easy to follow and it does not focus on the change itself. Instead, the model focuses on the approval and preparedness of the employees for the change, which facilitate an easier transition (Kotter 2012).

In conclusion, the models discussed in this chapter can guide managers or consultants as they lead or facilitate change. Figure 2-9 summarizes the key features, benefits, and limitations of these models. According to Burke and Litwin (1992) being well informed about the different change models reduces one's chances of becoming trapped by rigidly adhering to a single model.

A key point to remember is that OD consultants facilitate a process of applying diagnostic models to help the sponsor and the client diagnose their own problems. In AI there is no diagnosis because the OD consultant guides participants to discover organizational strengths and build on them. In change management, on the other hand, the consultant serves as the expert, and recommends solutions based on special knowledge.

A manager's tool titled An OD Action Research (AR) Checklist (see Appendix 1) is also provided. This tool can guide practitioners and consultants when implementing an AR approach to organizational change.

Figure 2-9. Key Features, Benefits, and Limitations of OD and CM Models

7-S Model Elements	Key Feature	Benefits	Limitations
Action Research (OD)	Model is grounded in a participatory, democratic worldview and concerned with developing practical knowledge. Major steps are planning, action, observation, and reflection before revising the plan.	• Used by practitioners • Collaborative and participative aimed at changing situation • Evaluative and reflective	• Cannot test hypothesis • Cannot establish cause and effect relationship • Cannot be generalized
Evolving Action Research Model (OD)	Interventions are considered to be happening like spirals rather than cycles. This represents their ongoing messy nature and the view that what is learned from each phase can be spun into subsequent phases.	• Freedom to undertake and adopt multiple objectives • Change takes on a process approach • Produces new behavior which helps process growth	• Also difficult to generalize and transfer

7-S Model Elements	Key Feature	Benefits	Limitations
Appreciative Inquiry (OD)	It is about the positive co-evolutionary search for the best in people and in organizations, with a focus on what is relevant in the world around them.	• Change from problem to possibility-focused • Restoration of hope, motivation, and commitment • Improved working relations and reduced conflict	• A focus on positives could invalidate the negative experiences and suppress potential solutions • What is positive for some may be negative for another—decontextualized polarization
McKinsey 7-S Model (CM)	Approach the organization holistically, to collectively determine how the organization operates.	• Parts are integral and must be attended to holistically • An effective method to diagnose and guide intervention • Contains rational and emotional components	• When one part changes, all parts change • Differences are ignored • Models are complex
Kotter's Eight-Step Change Model (CM)	Relate to management teams, individual responses, and approaches to change interventions in which people observe, make sense out of the process, and then change.	• Focus on buy-in of employees • Clear steps that guide the process • Suitable for hierarchical organizations	• Top-down model • Can lead to frustration among employees if individual needs are not considered.

Additional Reading

There are many more OD and CM models than those discussed in this chapter. The following are additional references to other models used to support the implementation of change in an organization.

- Weisbord's Six-Box Model is based on the book *Organizational Diagnosis: A Workbook of Theory and Practice*, by Marvin Weisbord.

- The Casual Model of Organizational Performance and Change is explained in the *Journal of Management* article "A Causal Model of Organizational Performance and Change" by Burke and Litwin.

- To learn more about the Institutional and Organizational (IOA) Model, check out the 2002 book *Organizational Assessment: A Framework for Improving Performance* by Lusthaus, Adrien, Anderson, Carden, and Montalvan.

- Leavitt's Model is detailed in Leavitt's 1965 chapter Applied Organizational Change in Industry in editor J. G. March's *Handbook of Organizations*.

- Likert System Analysis (1967) is best explained in Likert's 1967 book *The Human Organization: Its Management and Value*.

- Learn more about Congruence Model for Organization Analysis in: Nadler's and Tushman's 1980 article, A Model for Diagnosing Organizational Behavior from *Organizational Dynamics*.

- Tichy's Technical Political Cultural (TPC) Framework is explained in Tichy's 1983 book *Managing Strategic Change: Technical, Political, and Cultural Dynamics*.

- High-Performance Programming is detailed in Nelson and Burns' 1984 article High Performance Programming: A Framework for Transforming Organizations, in editor J. Adams' *Transforming Work*.

- Learn about Diagnosing Individual and Group Behavior in Harrison's 1987 book *Diagnosing Organizations: Methods, Models, and Processes*.

- The Burke-Litwin Model of Organizational Performance and Change is explained in Burke and Litwin's 1992 article, A Causal Model of Organizational Performance and Change in the *Journal of Management*.

3
The Organization Development Process

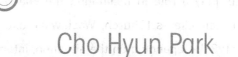

Cho Hyun Park

This chapter describes the process of change in OD. More specifically, it:
- explains the difference between internal and external OD consultants
- describes the step-by-step process of change.

Internal Versus External OD Consultants

Chapter 2 introduced several different models for change. Although there are some differences, all change processes go through the following six steps (see Figure 3-1):

1. entering and contracting
2. diagnosing and providing feedback
3. designing interventions
4. implementing
5. evaluating
6. institutionalizing or separating.

Figure 3-1. Change Process in Organization Development

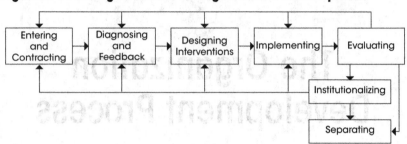

OD consultants play a role in facilitating the change process by collaborating with their clients (Church, Waclawski, and Burke 1996; Lippitt and Lippitt 1986). Depending on the situation, internal or external consultants are engaged in the change process, and when necessary internal and external consultants work in partnership (Scott and Barnes 2011). An internal OD consultant performs the OD practitioner's role as a full-time employee of the client organization. On the other hand, an external OD consultant belongs to another organization that usually provides consulting services. In this case, the client organization often hires an external consultant with a specialty or different perspective not possessed by internal consultants (Cummings and Worley 2008; Kurpius and Fuqua 1993). Although internal and external consultants both help their clients control change processes, their roles are different at each step of the process (Cummings and Worley 2008; Lacey 1995; Scott 2008; Weiss 2010). Before talking about each step in the OD change process, it is helpful to discuss the similarities and differences between internal and external consultants.

Internal consultants have the following advantages and disadvantages (Anderson 2012; Cummings and Worley 2008; Scott 2008; Scott and Barnes 2011; Weiss 2010).

- Advantages to using internal consultants:

  » They are members of the client organization, they are familiar with the organization's culture, systems, structures, and history. Thus, they are ready to be engaged in the change process and suited to dealing with sensitive issues.

  » They have already built relationships with organizational members and gained their trust. They can easily establish rapport, collaborate with the client, and immediately provide proper support, such as giving advice and coaching.

  » They can be involved in a long-term change process at a relatively low cost, because they are paid a salary rather than receiving an hourly payment like an external consultant.

  » The client organization's confidential issues will be safe.

- Disadvantages to using internal consultants:

  » They are too familiar with the organizational culture; they may not be able to view problems neutrally and objectively.

  » They may not be knowledgeable beyond the boundary of the organization and may lack particular knowledge, skills, or experience.

  » They may sometimes feel uncomfortable telling the truth and may find it difficult to face and handle unethical situations if they occur.

  » They may have difficulty building a client-consultant relationship due to their position or status in the organization. Employees may see them as HR, and senior executives may regard them as subordinates rather than consultants.

  » They have little choice about clients and projects.

External consultants also have advantages and disadvantages (Anderson 2012; Cummings and Worley 2008; Scott and Barnes 2011):

- Advantages to using external consultants:

  » Because they work for various client organizations, they have extensive experience and knowledge.

  » They can enter a change process in the client organization with less internal political bias.

  » If members of an organization perceive the consultants as outsiders who are not involved in the organization's political issues, they are more likely to share their confidential views and honest opinions.

  » They may find it easier to reject unethical situations and maintain neutrality and objectivity.

  » They can have power as change process experts.

  » They can select clients or projects based on their own criteria.

- Disadvantages to using external consultants:

  » They may sometimes be unable to understand the client organization's language or ulterior motives in issues.

  » It may take time to establish rapport with members of the client organization and gain members' trust.

  » They are perceived as engaged in the change process over the short term, and may not be able to follow up on the change process in the long term.

You must understand the situation and weigh the advantages and disadvantages of either internal or external consultants for each change process. For some situations a partnership between internal and external consultants that combines their advantages may bring better results (Cummings and Worley 2008; Scott and Barnes 2011).

Marketing

Marketing is especially important for external OD consultants because it provides information about services and consulting fees to prospective clients. Even internal OD consultants should market their capabilities to remind top management how they contribute to organizational performance (Weiss 2010). Therefore, although marketing itself is not a direct part of a change process, it is essential for a consultant to do.

Those engaged in successful marketing understand market needs, realize their strengths as a consultant, and possess a passion for OD consulting (Weiss 2010). Similar to other industries, OD consulting should reflect the customer's changing needs. Initially, clients primarily sought to use OD to instill humanism in their organizations, but these needs have changed and today's clients ask OD consultants to enhance organizational effectiveness in various ways (Krell 1981). History is replete with examples of industry decline due to marketing myopia and an overall inability to meet the customer's changing needs. A notable example is the railroad industry. Railroad companies failed to meet the needs of their customers because they only defined themselves as railroad businesses. If they had seen themselves as a transportation business instead, they may have met their customers' expectations for faster, more flexible, more durable, and cheaper transportation (Levitt 1960).

OD consultants need to advertise their competencies and consulting experiences to attract clients (Weiss 2010). Chapter 4 discusses the essential competencies OD consultants need to master to be successful.

Finally, a passionate commitment (Adams 2003) and enthusiasm (Hamilton 1988) are vital to successful OD consulting, since, without passion, consultants may not be motivated or fully engaged in the change process (Weiss 2010). This is especially important at the marketing stage, because OD consultants must show their passion to prospective clients.

There are many ways for external consultants to market their consulting services, including:

- Previous client recommendations: Clients who have a successful experience will recommend the OD consultants' service to others. This is the most common and effective way an external consultant can get new clients.

- Network: External consultants can use their social network and social media to look for new clients.

- Prior employers: External consultants can also receive work or referrals from previous employers.

- Websites: Websites provide information about the consultant that prospective clients would want to know.

- Printed materials: A business card is an effective way to communicate professionally.

- Request for proposals (RFPs): A well-written proposal in response to RFPs can show that a consultant is qualified.

- Referrals from or work with associates: If consultant's colleagues are involved in a project that is too big for them to handle, they may make a referral for the consultant.

- Previous clients: A consultant may have opportunities to work with previous clients again.

- Visibility: Publications, such as books, articles, or presentations may attract the attention of prospective clients.

- Contract agencies: This approach may be helpful when a consulting market is tight.

- Pro-bono work: By consulting for free or at a reduced fee, a consultant can demonstrate expertise and market his or her professional services (McLean 2006).

Entering

Usually, a change process in OD starts with identifying issues that the organization wants to improve or resolve. Then the organization selects internal or external OD consultants with whom to work.

An external consultant should decide whether or not to work for a project or client based on his or her own criteria. After making an affirmative decision, the consultant will need to establish relationships with members of the organization and learn about the company's jargon, systems, structure, and culture.

For an internal consultant, the entering step is easier because he or she will not need to select a client, create relationships, or learn about the company (Lacey 1995). The internal consultant is already a member of the organization and therefore knows about it and its members.

Contracting

After deciding to work with a client or on a project, the next step that an OD consultant should take is contracting (Raab 2013). The contract is usually a written agreement outlining expectations for consulting, as well as mutual consent for both parties' engagement in the change process (Block 2011). An external OD consultant needs to sign a formal written contract with the client company. By contrast, an internal OD consultant may not need a formal contract and may make an informal or oral contract instead (Lacey 1995). A contract typically includes the following items:

- project objectives
- boundaries of consulting
- the roles of the client and the consultant
- expected outcomes
- timeline and available resources
- deliverables
- ground rules including
  » what to keep confidential

- » how to deal with personal or interpersonal issues
- » to what extent the consultant helps the client
- » how to terminate the client-consultant relationship
- a fee (external consultant) or extra pay/benefit (internal consultant) (Block 2011; Cummings and Worley 2008; Scott and Barnes 2011) and terms of payment.

Diagnosing

The entering and contracting step is followed by the second step of the OD change process—diagnosing organizations. An accurate diagnosis shows what is happening in the organization and suggests proper interventions to resolve or improve organizational issues (Cummings and Worley 2008; Lundberg 2008).

The term diagnosis is one you frequently hear in a hospital. If you do not feel healthy, you will visit a doctor, and the doctor will diagnose your symptoms and give you a prescription to improve your health. However, in OD the term diagnosis is used differently. In OD, the client and the consultant collaborate in diagnosing organizational issues and seeking solutions, whereas the medical doctor diagnoses a patient and writes up a prescription unilaterally (Cummings and Worley 2008). OD diagnosis is a collaborative process of clarifying organizational issues and gaining an analytic understanding of identified issues. The diagnosis process enables the client and consultant to make sense of the change process (Lundberg 2008).

Three factors make OD diagnosis successful: processes, models, and methods (Harrison 2005). The OD diagnosis is a process through which the client and consultant create a collaborative and constructive relationship, which will have a significant effect on the diagnosis results. Even though the project is defined at the contracting step, some issues should be redefined during the diagnosis process. OD consultants should manage the following issues in order to maintain a collaborative and constructive relationship:

- Purpose: What is the goal of this project?
- Design: How will data gathering affect organization members?
- Support and cooperation: Who is the sponsor, the client, or the stakeholder? Who will support this project and what resources will be available?
- Participation: What are the roles of each party in the diagnosis process?
- Feedback: When, how, and for whom will the feedback be provided? (Harrison 2005; Van de Ven and Ferry 1980)

A diagnostic model also helps the OD consultant frame and define problems, collect and analyze data, and provide feedback (Harrison 2005). As explained in chapter 2, from the OD perspective, organizations are viewed as living systems that change and evolve (Jaros and Dostal 1995). An organization is a system composed of sub-systems, such as groups, teams, work units, or individuals, and systems theory provides a framework that can help the consultant understand the organization holistically and can suggest methodologies for diagnosing the organization as a system. The open systems model is a diagnostic model based on systems theory (Cummings and Worley 2008). According to this model, an organization that functions within an external environment transforms certain inputs from its environment into outputs. The outputs act as feedback in this transformation process. This open system model can be applied at individual, group, and organizational levels, allowing diagnosis to occur at each level.

Selecting appropriate methods can ensure successful diagnosis because the right methods bring valid and reliable results (Harrison 2005). Methods should be selected in light of the client's organizational culture. For example, to diagnose an organization in which most employees are engaged in emotional labor, qualitative methodologies such as observation or interview might be appropriate to gather empathic data. To select appropriate methodologies, it is important to know the pros and cons of each. The next section looks at commonly used data-gathering methodologies.

Data Gathering

OD consultants should collect data to diagnose organizational issues and seek appropriate interventions based on their analysis of data results. OD consultants can choose to gather qualitative data, quantitative data, or a combination of the two (Waclawski and Church 2002). Qualitative data can be collected through observation, interviews, or focus groups; quantitative data can be collected through surveys, assessments, or performance measurement. Among these data-gathering methodologies, questionnaires, observations, interviews, and secondary data are the most commonly used.

It is important for external consultants to build rapport and trust with their clients to obtain credible data. On the other hand, because internal consultants have already formed relationships with the organization's members, they can often gather truthful data more easily (Lacey 1995).

Providing Feedback

After analyzing the data gathered in collaboration with the client, the consultant should give the client feedback. This provides information about the organization's current situation and motivates organizational members to participate in a change process that involves designing interventions, implementation, evaluation, and institutionalizing steps. When OD consultants provide feedback, they have to keep in mind who, what, where, when, why, and how.

- Who should receive feedback? People can have confidence in the change process and be motivated to actively participate in that change process by receiving feedback (Warrick 2010). Therefore, OD consultants should provide feedback for everyone involved in the change process to let them know where they are and how they should move forward.

- What should the feedback include? Because the results will be used to plan actions that the client should take to resolve or improve organizational issues, the relevant and significant information should be summarized and presented. Also, because the interventions will be designed and developed based on the feedback, the data presented should be accurate. However, because people cannot absorb too much information at once, only the necessary information should be provided (Cummings and Worley 2008).

- Where should the feedback be provided? Gathering in one physical place is the most effective way to deliver the feedback, because the audience's questions can be answered on the spot. However, in a large organization this may not be possible. In this case, the cascading approach or written format can also be used (McLean 2006).

- When should the feedback be provided? The feedback should be provided as soon as possible (Cummings and Worley 2008). If the data are provided too late, people may forget they were involved in the data collection process and may not be interested in the feedback. If this happens, the feedback cannot draw attention from organizational members and may be less effective in motivating them to participate in the succeeding change process.

- Why should the feedback be provided? The primary purpose of the feedback is to encourage people to actively participate in the change process. It acts as a stimulus to discussion, decision making, and action planning to resolve or improve organizational issues (Cummings and Worley 2008; Harrison

2005). Sometimes the feedback may make both the feedback provider and recipients uncomfortable. However, the change process can proceed when people are ready to accept the feedback (Folkman 2006).

- How should the feedback be provided? The data provided should be understandable to the audience. The use of graphs, charts, tables, or examples can help people better understand the data (Cummings and Worley 2008).

Sometimes the feedback step is regarded as less important than other steps and even skipped. However, it is important because it encourages members of the client organization to actively participate in the change process. People who are fully motivated are more willing to come up with their own solutions to organizational issues.

Although the roles of external and internal consultants are quite similar, there are some differences in terms of their status as consultants. An external consultant who has prestige as an outside specialist can use his authority to structure meetings and choose the appropriate members to attend the meetings. On the other hand, because an internal consultant is also a member of the organization, her status depends on her position in the organization. Thus, it may be difficult for her to arrange meetings or appoint people to attend the meetings. An internal consultant may also experience difficulties in encouraging people to confront sensitive organizational issues rather than avoiding them (Lacey 1995).

Designing Interventions

The diagnostic procedure is followed by the goal-setting and action-planning step (Lippitt and Lippitt 1986). Once the client group becomes aware of the problems or opportunities, they have to decide how to move forward. The client group and the consultant should have a clear idea about what they want or need, what they have to be, and their value. In doing so, realistic and attainable goals can be set, and effective interventions to resolve or improve organizational issues can be devised.

After setting goals, specific interventions should be designed to achieve them. The term *intervention* means a series of actions planned for an organization, groups, or individuals to achieve their effectiveness or improvement (French and Bell 1999). An effective intervention should address the organizational needs determined by the diagnosis step, be based on the confidence that the intended outcome will be achieved, and be able to enhance organizational capacity to control their own change (Cummings and Worley 2008). By designing interventions in collaboration with the client, members of the client organization can be motivated and mobilized to implement the interventions (Warrick 2010).

Because time, money, and human resources are used to develop interventions, the intended outcomes should be achieved through the interventions. To develop successful interventions, OD consultants should:

- Focus on problems or opportunities that may be resolved or enhanced through the interventions.
- Involve the people who may be affected by the problems or opportunities with which the intervention deals.
- Clarify the goals that should be achieved through the interventions.
- Have realistic and attainable expectations of success.
- Contain both experiential and conceptual learning.
- Create an environment in which people feel free to learn.
- Design activities through which people learn how to solve problems and how to learn.
- Create activities through which people learn both tasks and processes.

- Structure activities through which people or sub-units can be integrated as a whole (French and Bell 1999).

A pilot simulation is very important for ensuring the successful outcomes of the interventions. Through this process, it is possible to anticipate who should be involved and how to create strategies for engaging the relevant people (Lippitt and Lippitt 1986).

OD interventions deal with a broad range of problems or opportunities from the individual level to team/group and organizational levels. At the individual level, OD interventions focus on the individual job or position and are used to improve individual effectiveness, such as individual job performance, satisfaction, and development. Intervention examples include coaching, mentoring, job design, conflict management, and leadership development. At the team or group level, OD interventions focus on group dynamics and are designed to improve team or group effectiveness, such as performance and quality of work-life within a team or group. Team building, process consultation, team conflict resolution, and meeting facilitation are typical examples of team- or group-level interventions. Organizational OD interventions are designed to increase organizational performance and productivity, stakeholder satisfaction, and similar. Organization design, culture change, accountability and reward systems, succession planning, and strategic planning are examples of OD interventions at the organizational level (Cummings and Worley 2008; McLean 2006). In chapter 5, OD interventions are explained in more detail.

OD consultants should encourage members of the client organization to take part in designing the implementation step. Internal consultants may find this advantageous because they know what resources can be involved, however, it might be difficult for them to involve top management, depending on their position or status within the organization.

External consultants, on the other hand, can easily induce top management to commit to the change process due to their prestige as experts in the OD field (Lippitt and Lippitt 1986).

Implementing

Once the interventions are designed, they need to be implemented. In order to attain the desired outcomes for the identified organizational issues, all relevant employees should participate in the interventions. To successfully manage this step, OD consultants should keep the following process in mind:

1. Develop a clear vision.
   - Identify the core value and purpose of the organization.
   - Describe the future that members of the organization want to create.
2. Take a broad view of the change process.
   - Keep the ultimate goal of the change process in mind.
   - See the organization as a whole system.
3. Motivate organizational members to be engaged.
   - Help people be ready to change.
   - Keep people actively involved in the change process.
   - Determine reasons for any resistance to change and ways to overcome them.
4. Manage the change process.
   - Adopt a proper change model.
   - Create activity planning and commitment planning.
   - Select appropriate interventions.
   - Learn how to change through the change process.

5. Manage the political dynamics of change to derive support.

   • Identify the source of change agent power.

   • Clarify key stakeholders to get their support.

6. Maintain impetus.

   • Refuel extra resources additionally required for change.

   • Create a system to provide psychological and emotional support.

   • Reinforce new competencies needed to implement the change.

   • Stay focused on the change process until it is completely implemented (Cummings and Worley 2008; Warrick 2010).

In implementation, the main role of the consultant is to help people learn the appropriate knowledge and skills needed for the success of their change process. The consultant should also praise all successes achieved during the change process, because doing so motivates people toward achieving their goals. An internal consultant may find it easier to observe members' activities and help them gain the appropriate knowledge and skills required for the successful implementation. On the other hand, an external consultant with experiences in many other organizations can bring in diverse activities to help people develop the skills required (Lippitt and Lippitt 1986).

Evaluating

Evaluation is a continuing process. While it should occur during the intervention, it is also important after implementing the intervention to evaluate whether the change effort was effective. OD is a learning process through which people can learn how to assess organizational issues, how to resolve the issues assessed, and how to implement the solution devised. By evaluating the change process, people will determine whether it was successful and will decide whether to undertake another change process (Morrison 1978). The evaluation step of the change process involves assessing the progress and impact of the interventions (Cady, Auger, and Foxon 2010). The evaluation offers information about institutionalizing, keeping or expanding successful interventions, and adjusting or abandoning inadequate ones (Thomas 2005).

Although the evaluation process provides critical information, it is not easy for the following reasons:

- Evaluation should be carefully planned in the early stage of the change process. If not, it may be impossible to evaluate the change process correctly.

- Clients may consider evaluation to be a waste of time and money.

- When the outcomes of the change process are not satisfactory, OD consultants or clients may be unwilling to conduct an evaluation.

- It is difficult to measure the outcome of interventions.

- It could be impossible to separate the effects of interventions from the effects of something else happening in an organization (Scott and Barnes 2011).

Evaluations should be conducted to lead the change effort to success. Even if evaluation results show that the change process was not successful, they can still provide a direction to follow to ultimately make the change effort successful.

The evaluation can be conducted based on the following four-step process (Cady, Auger, and Foxon 2010):

1. Develop an evaluation plan. In this step, the OD consultant should identify the purpose and outcomes of the evaluation because people will not be willing to participate in this step without convincing reasons. The consultant must consider the people who will be involved; the action plan, which includes what evaluation model and measures will be used, how to

collect and analyze data; how to report the evaluation results; and the resources available, such as time, money, and facilities as well as support.

2. Conduct the evaluation. Although a sound evaluation plan results in a favorable evaluation process, it is possible that something unexpected will come out of it, too. Therefore, factors that could arise should be anticipated in advance.

3. Report the evaluation results. To effectively deliver the evaluation results to key stakeholders, the results should be presented clearly. Various tools can be used for effective reporting, such as charts, graphs, scorecards, stories, or pictures.

4. Learn through the evaluation process. People can experience and practice the evaluation process, including data collection and analysis, decision-making and judgment, and future planning. Doing so can improve the client's ability to evaluate the change process.

As diverse interventions are being implemented to handle identified organizational issues, various evaluation approaches can be used. This chapter introduces five evaluation approaches that can be easily applied to practice: Kirkpatrick's four levels of evaluation, return on investment, balanced scorecard, dashboard, and key performance indicators.

Kirkpatrick's Four Levels of Evaluation

One of the most famous and popular models is Kirtpatrick's Four Levels of Evaluation model (Kirkpatrick and Kirkpatrick 2006). The training should be measured at four levels:

- Level 1: Reaction. This level of evaluation is to measure how people feel about the training program they attended. Usually, a survey method is used to measure trainees' satisfaction.

- Level 2: Learning. This level involves evaluating what knowledge, skills, attitudes, or behaviors were acquired through the training program. A written test or demonstration is commonly used to evaluate the degree of learning. Observation or interviews can also be used.

- Level 3: Behavior. This level is included to evaluate the improvement of trainee behavior on the job and their ability to implement what they learned. This can be measured through an interview with the trainee or observations by the trainee's supervisor, training practitioners, or from the self-assessment.

- Level 4: Results. In this level, the impact of the training program on the business is evaluated. For this level of evaluation, various bottom-line measures can be used.

Kirkpatrick's evaluation model is widely practiced because it is easy to use and understand. In addition, the evaluation occurs from a system perspective because it measures performance from the individual level to the business level. However, this evaluation model lacks research-based theoretical support. Use of the term *level* is also somewhat inaccurate because the link between one level and the next is unclear. Most of all, it may not be suitable for some OD interventions because this model was originally devised to evaluate the effects of training programs (McLean 2006).

Return on Investment (ROI)

ROI is "the ultimate measure of accountability that answers the question: Is there a financial return for investing in a program, process, initiative, or performance improvement solution?" (Phillips and Phillips 2005, 1). ROI can be calculated using the following equation:

ROI (%) = (Net Program Benefits ÷ Program Costs) × 100

Let's say, for example, that you spend $2,000 for an intervention and you get back $5,000. In this case, the net program benefit is $3,000, and the program cost is $2,000. Therefore, ROI is 150%, or ($3,000 ÷ $2,000) × 100.

However, ROI alone is not sufficient for reporting performance, so it is more meaningful when it is reported with other performance measures. For instance, ROI can be added as the fifth level to Kirkpatrick's four levels of evaluation:

- Level 1: Reaction and satisfaction

- Level 2: Learning

- Level 3: Application and implementation

- Level 4: Business impact

- Level 5: ROI.

By adding the monetary benefit term, more comprehensive performance information can be obtained. However, it is difficult to isolate the impact of the intervention when ROI is used as an evaluation approach (Phillips and Phillips 2005).

Balanced Scorecard (BSC)

BSC is "a set of measures that gives top managers a fast, but comprehensive, view of the business. The balanced scorecard includes financial measures that tell the results of actions already taken. And it complements the financial measures with operational measures on customer satisfaction, internal processes, and the organization's innovation and improvement activities—operational measures that are the drivers of future financial performance" (Kaplan and Norton 1992, 71). BSC measures financial and nonfinancial performance from four perspectives: financial, customer, internal business, and innovation and learning (Kaplan and Norton 1992, 1996).

- Financial perspective: How should we achieve financial performance to satisfy shareholders?

- Customer perspective: How should we satisfy our customers?

- Internal business perspective: What internal business process should we focus on to achieve shareholder and customer satisfaction?
- Innovation and learning perspective: How can we keep changing and improving to fulfill our value?

BSC is a strategic evaluation approach that focuses on continuous change and measures financial performance, which is the main concern of top management. However, because BSC focuses on the impacts at the organizational level, it may need to be modified to capture valuable data at lower levels to show business impact on key performance indicators. In addition, equal weight is attached to the four measures although each measure may have different impact on the change process (Chytas, Glykas, and Valiris 2011).

Dashboard

A performance dashboard is like a car dashboard, which panoptically displays key information essential for safe driving, such as speed, fuel, and engine temperature. A performance dashboard also shows key performance indicators—it is "a visual display of the most important information needed to achieve one or more objectives; consolidated and arranged on a single screen so the information can be monitored at a glance" (Few 2004, 15).

There is no fixed format for a dashboard. However, when drawing one, the most important rule is to concisely display performance measures with colorful graphic indicators or gauges to help influence an intuitive understanding of progress. The dashboard is very popular, due to its simplicity, flexibility, and ease of use, but it may not provide enough information. Therefore, the dashboard should be designed to clearly and effectively display key performance indicators (Few 2006).

Every evaluation approach has both strengths and weaknesses, so it is up to the OD consultant to facilitate a way for the client to select the best approach. No matter what the OD consultants use, it is very important to establish an evaluation plan before implementing any OD intervention. A well planned and implemented evaluation process enables a rigorous assessment of the OD intervention's outcomes (Livingston 2006).

In the evaluation step, internal consultants are able to provide feedback from the organizational strategic standpoint. They should avoid hiding problems or feeding selective information back to organizational members, and be ready to help them understand the information. Internal consultants can observe the process involved in institutionalizing change efforts and offer long-term help. Conversely, external consultants sometimes leave the client organization before the institutionalizing step. They may be more knowledgeable about new evaluation approaches, however, and can easily call official feedback sessions with key stakeholders (Lacey 1995; Lippitt and Lippitt 1986).

Institutionalizing

Institutionalization is "a process for maintaining a particular change for an appropriate period of time" (Cummings and Worley 2008, 189). Because the change should assimilate into the organizational culture (Buchanan et al. 2005), institutionalization is important for guaranteeing the long-term success of change efforts (Jacobs 2002).

An institutionalization framework should include organization and intervention characteristics, institutionalization processes, and indicators of institutionalization (Cummings and Worley 2008).

- Organization characteristics are factors that influence intervention characteristics and institutionalization processes.

  » Congruence: The extent to which an intervention is aligned with the organizational mission, values, strategy, or structures.

  » Stability of environment and technology: The extent to which the organizational environment and technology are stable.

  » Unionization: The extent to which the organization is unionized. In a highly unionized organization interventions may be difficult.

- Intervention characteristics are dimensions that impact the institutionalization process.

  » Goal specificity: The intervention goal should be concrete and clear.

  » Programmability: The change program must be designed to enable institutionalization.

  » Level of change target: The change target should be specified.

  » Internal support: The extent to which the change process is supported internally.

  » Sponsorship: The extent to which sponsorship is powerful enough to control resources for the intervention.

- Institutionalization processes are the ways OD interventions are integrated into the organization.

  » Socialization: The propagation of beliefs, norms, and values underlying the intervention.

  » Commitment: The engagement of members in the intervention.

  » Reward allocation: The reward system for acquiring the behaviors desired for the intervention.

  » Diffusion: The spread of change between systems in the organization.

» Sensing and calibration: Perceiving the factors that affect institutionalized behaviors and adjusting the behaviors.

- Indicators of institutionalization refer to the persistence of the change.

  » Knowledge: Members understand the behaviors required by the intervention.

  » Performance: The actions required by the intervention are taken.

  » Preferences: Members positively take the change.

  » Normative consensus: Members think that the change is appropriate.

  » Value consensus: Members agree about the value of the change.

Internal OD consultants can keep observing the institutionalization process in the long term whereas external consultants are usually separated from the client organization after accomplishing what they agreed to achieve at the contracting step. However, external consultants can periodically follow up on the institutionalization of change efforts. This may be a better way to objectively see the institutionalizing status, because external consultants do not share the institutionalizing process within the organization, whereas internal consultants experience it along with the organizational members (McLean 2006).

Separating

Separating is the last step. The consultant and the client review the contract that was signed at the beginning of the change process and decide whether the consultant will continue the change process or leave the client organization (Van Eron and Burke 2010). There are several ways to separate from a client organization:

- Train the members of the client organization to keep managing the change process and hand over functions managed by the consultant.

- Gradually decrease the consultant's involvement.

- Have a commemoration to celebrate the collaborative change effort.

- Make a minimal follow-up plan (Lippitt and Lippitt 1986).

Although this is the end of the change process, it is very important to have a good ending that satisfies both parties. If the separating step is skipped, people may think the change process just fizzled out. In addition, people may not have the opportunity to transform the implicit knowledge they learned through change efforts to explicit knowledge that is articulated, codified, and stored in some format. A good ending is also advantageous to external consultants, who are always seeking to acquire good reputations. The clients may want to work with the consultants again in the future and may also be willing to recommend them to other clients (McLean 2006).

Worksheet 3-1: Check Yourself

Direction: At each phase of the OD process, use this checklist to see how you are doing. It provides a list of items to keep in mind at each phase.		
Phase	Questions	Response
Entering and Contracting	1. Did you identify objectives and boundaries of consulting?	Yes ☐ No ☐
	2. Did you clarify the roles of client and consultant?	Yes ☐ No ☐
	3. Did you stipulate expected outcomes for the project?	Yes ☐ No ☐
	4. Did you identify available resources and determine a timeline?	Yes ☐ No ☐
	5. Did you set ground rules for the whole OD process?	Yes ☐ No ☐
	6. Did you set and contract for a fee if you are an external consultant or for extra benefit if you are an internal consultant?	Yes ☐ No ☐

Phase	Questions	Response
Diagnosing	1. Are you aware of the goal of this project?	Yes ☐ No ☐
	2. Did you plan for data collection?	Yes ☐ No ☐
	3. Did you identify sponsor, client, or stakeholders and clarify who will support and who will collaborate on the project?	Yes ☐ No ☐
	4. Did you determine the roles of each party in the diagnosing process?	Yes ☐ No ☐
	5. Did you plan when, how, and for whom you will provide feedback?	Yes ☐ No ☐
Designing	1. Does the intervention design focus on resolving the identified problem?	Yes ☐ No ☐
	2. Did you involve the relevant people who may be affected by the problems or opportunities involved?	Yes ☐ No ☐
	3. Did you set realistic and attainable goals that should be achieved through the intervention?	Yes ☐ No ☐
	4. Were proper learning environments created?	Yes ☐ No ☐
	5. Does the intervention include proper activities through which people can learn how to resolve problems?	Yes ☐ No ☐
Implementing	1. Did you specify the organization's core value with which the intervention should be aligned?	Yes ☐ No ☐
	2. Do you see the organization as a whole system and everything happening in the organization as a change process from a broad perspective?	Yes ☐ No ☐
	3. Do you have a specific plan to motivate people engaged in the change process?	Yes ☐ No ☐
	4. Did you identify the source of power and key stakeholders to get support?	Yes ☐ No ☐
	5. Do you have a plan to maintain impetus for the continuous change process?	Yes ☐ No ☐

Phase	Questions	Response
Evaluating	1. Did you identify who will be involved in the evaluation process?	Yes ☐ No ☐
	2. Did you decide which evaluation model/ measures to use?	Yes ☐ No ☐
	3. Did you identify available resources in the evaluation process?	Yes ☐ No ☐
	4. Did you plan for the collection and analysis of data?	Yes ☐ No ☐
	5. Did you plan when, how, and for whom you will report the evaluation results?	Yes ☐ No ☐
	6. Did organizational members acquire a proper ability through the evaluation process to conduct an evaluation by themselves?	Yes ☐ No ☐

4

Competencies of Organization Development Consultants

Cho Hyun Park

"A competent portraitist knows how to imply the profile in the full face."
—Aldous Huxley, English novelist and critic

This chapter discusses the competencies that OD consultants require to:
- perform their role
- adapt in today's rapidly changing environment.

Competencies for the OD Consultant's Role

Competency, in general terms, means "an organism's capacity to interact effectively with its environment" (White 1959, 297). This definition can be applied to human beings and can be interpreted as their capability to cope with any situation in which they are placed. Given that every organization is formed to accomplish certain goals, in an organizational setting, the competency of people assembled to achieve goals can be construed as

characteristics that individuals have and use in appropriate, consistent ways in order to achieve desired
performance. These characteristics include knowledge,
skills, aspects of self-image, social motives, traits,
thought patterns, mindsets, and ways of thinking, feeling, and acting. (Dubois and Rothwell 2004, 16)

The definition of competency can also be applied to job situations
and interpreted as an employee's individual characteristics required to
perform her job in a superior way.

Organization development consultants also need appropriate
competencies to perform their job in an effective way. OD competency can be defined as "any 'personal quality' that contributes to the
successful practice of OD" (Rothwell, Stavros, and Sullivan 2010, 6).
What specific quality should OD consultants possess? Before specifying
the competencies of OD consultants, it is necessary to consider what OD
consultants' roles are and what they do.

As emphasized in chapter 1, OD is a bottom-up change effort to
improve the relationships among organizational members in the long
term, whereas change management either refers to a top-down change
effort or is simply used as a marketing term, encompassing all ways
to change people. Because an OD approach is different from a change
management approach, an OD consultant is different from a change
management consultant (Bushe and Marshak 2009; Worren, Ruddle,
and Moore 1999).

The pivotal role of OD consultants is to facilitate change, rather than
to provide specific prescriptions as change management consultants do
(Church, Waclawski, and Burke 1996; Lippitt and Lippitt 1986; Worren,
Ruddle, and Moore 1999). As facilitators, OD consultants do not directly
control change efforts or recommend solutions. Rather, they collaborate with clients, help them control the change process by themselves,

and encourage participation to empower them to make decisions and solve problems based on OD values, humanism, optimism, and democracy (Burke 1994; French and Bell 1999). For example, to solve an employee tardiness problem, which could affect organizational performance, change management consultants may recommend modifying the system by adding a punishment or penalty. On the other hand, OD consultants may assist and advise employees in order to help them realize their own problems, figure out why, and come up with a solution.

No single qualification certifies the abilities of an OD consultant (Anderson 2012). Although much research has been conducted on OD competencies (Burke 1982; Church, Wadowski, and Burke 1996; Shepard and Raia 1981; Varney 1980; Worley and Feyerherm 2003; Worley, Rothwell, and Sullivan 2010; Worley and Varney 1998), the results of those studies have suggested different sets of required competencies for OD consultants. Nevertheless, it is very important to gain a good understanding of a specific competency model because of its utility as a self-reflection tool in diagnosing strengths and weaknesses (Worley, Rothwell, and Sullivan 2010). This chapter introduces the sets of competencies needed by OD consultants for successful organization development.

A survey of 364 OD professionals, who worked for private organizations in the United States and held master's degrees, was conducted to ask about the essential competencies for OD consultants. The survey revealed the importance of the following: self-mastery, comfort with ambiguity, managing transitions and institutionalization, collaboration in design, managing separation, managing client, accountability, setting the conditions for positive change, using data to adjust change, ability to work with large systems, tech savvy or awareness, ability to evaluate change, ability to clarify data needs, strong research methods, listening skills, building realistic expectations, ability to work with and manage diversity, ability to clarify roles, openmindedness, ability to see the whole picture, ability to integrate theory and practice, focus on flexibility, and clear communication (Worley, Rothwell, and Sullivan 2010).

The skills required for each step in a successful OD process, which you learned in chapter 3, were also determined:

- Marketing: Successfully describe OD processes, quickly assess opportunities for change, clarify outcomes and resources, develop relationships, and make good client choices.

- Start-up: Set the conditions for change, address power, build cooperative relationships, and clarify roles.

- Diagnosis/Feedback: Apply appropriate research methods, keep the information flowing, clarify data needs, keep an open mind regarding data, and focus on relevance.

- Action planning: Create an implementation plan, facilitate the action planning process, and obtain commitment from leadership.

- Intervention: Adjust implementation and transfer ownership of the change.

- Evaluation: Evaluate success of change and use the data to adjust the change.

- Adoption: Manage adoption and institutionalization.

- Separation: Manage the transition.

Other competencies included the ability to master self, be available to multiple stakeholders, work with large-scale clients, manage diversity, be current in theory and technology, maintain a flexible focus, possess broad facilitation skills, and be comfortable with ambiguity (Worley, Rothwell, and Sullivan 2010).

There was also an attempt to classify competencies required for OD consultants into three areas:

- Foundation competencies
  - » knowledge of organization behavior including culture, ethics, psychology, and leadership
  - » individual psychology
  - » group dynamics
  - » management and organization theory and design
  - » research methods/statistics
  - » comparative cultural perspectives
  - » functional knowledge of business.
- Knowledge competencies
  - » organization design and research
  - » system dynamics
  - » history of OD and change
  - » theories and models for change.
- Skill competencies
  - » managing the consulting process
  - » analysis and diagnosis
  - » designing and choosing appropriate and relevant interventions
  - » facilitation and process consultation
  - » developing client capability
  - » evaluating organization change (Worley and Varney 1998).

OD is a complex field that covers a wide range of areas, including psychology, sociology, anthropology, group dynamics, organizational behaviors, management, and systems theory (French and Bell 1999; Waclawski and Church 2002), and as a result, OD practitioners have diverse backgrounds and experiences (Anderson 2012; Bunker, Alban, and Lewicki 2004; Lippitt and Lippitt 1986). While OD consultants have their own individual areas of change specialization, they still need to understand the basic competencies as a starting point in their ongoing development (Worley, Rothwell, and Sullivan 2010). Therefore consultants can advance in the OD consulting field by making steady and persistent efforts to bolster their strengths and make up for their weaknesses.

Today's Rapid Changes and OD Competencies

When the term organization development emerged in the 1950s, its focus was on group dynamics. The OD field has been evolving, however, and its focus has broadened (French and Bell 1999; Worley and Feyerherm 2003; Worley, Rothwell, and Sullivan 2010). Today OD refers to a long-term change effort focused on improving issues related to the interpersonal relationships of organizational members. The world is experiencing rapid changes, and organizations need to be prepared to cope with them (Eoyang 2010).

What would happen if OD competencies do not change even though the field keeps maturing and the organizational environment keeps evolving? Could consultants keep helping clients manage their change processes effectively? The aforementioned competencies are necessary for OD consultants to perform their basic role, but may not be enough to deal with uncertain rapid changes. Thus, preparing for an unpredictable future may be a challenge for OD consultants.

Organization development has been affected by global trends including concentrated wealth, globalization, ecological concern, diverse workforce, advances in technology, and the networked and knowledge-based organization. Thus, OD practitioners may find it helpful to learn which OD competencies may be required to handle any impacts from these trends. Based on a survey of 21 OD master's degree students, 16 themes were identified relating to OD competencies required for dealing with the changes in economy, workforce, technology, and organizations (Worley and Feyerherm 2003, 105):

- large systems fluency
- diplomacy in tough situations
- ability to design and revise systems
- strong leadership
- understanding of business and line management
- broad understanding of the world
- see how systems operate as a whole
- research and evaluation skills
- breadth of fieldwork and experience in the field
- self-knowledge and exploration
- deep understanding of an organization
- use and develop new models of change and organization
- embrace various perspectives across cultures
- collaboration
- thorough knowledge about the OD field
- conviction about the OD practice.

In 2013, in light of the unpredictable economic climate, the evolution of learning technology, the generational shift in workforce, and the globalization of the business world, ATD revised its competency model for training and development (T&D) professionals. This competency model is composed of two parts: areas of expertise and foundational competencies. Areas of expertise are the specific knowledge and actions required for T&D professionals to perform their roles, and foundational competencies are the base for specialized knowledge and skills (Arneson, Rothwell, and Naughton 2013).

The ATD Competency Model lists six foundational competencies: business skills, global mindset, industry knowledge, interpersonal skills, personal skills, and technology literacy.

These foundational competencies are required not only for T&D professionals but also for all professionals in learning and performance, including OD practitioners. Acquiring these foundational competencies will assist OD practitioners in becoming capable learning and performance professionals in today's rapidly changing business environment.

Although this chapter introduced many of the competencies required by OD consultants, it is nearly impossible to have command of all of them. The competency list is provided as a way to help guide your ongoing development as an OD consultant (McLean 2006). While some competencies are inherent characteristics, others can be developed through continuous learning (White 1959). You simply need to identify your strengths and weaknesses as an OD consultant and steadily improve your competencies to increase your success and move forward in the OD field.

Worksheet 4-1. Check Yourself

Direction: Although this chapter introduced insights into the competencies of OD consultants, these may differ depending on organizational characteristics, environments, situations, and so forth. Based on the competencies introduced in this chapter, think about your strengths and weaknesses as an internal or external OD consultant. Then, make a plan to improve your competencies.

1. What are your strengths as an OD consultant?

2. What are your weaknesses as an OD consultant?

3. What barriers hinder you from improving your competencies and how can you overcome these obstacles?

4. Describe a step-by-step plan to promote your competencies as an OD consultant.

5
Implementation of Organization Development

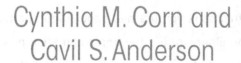

Cynthia M. Corn and
Cavil S. Anderson

"The implementation phase is the core of an organization's change effort.

It is the movement and transition to another state of being and operation."
—W. Warner Burke in Rothwell (2005, 313)

This chapter focuses on:

- traditional ways of implementing OD
- exercises that can be used individually or in groups to apply the various implementation concepts
- examples of how you can apply theory to real life situations.

Anyone who has been in business in the United States has heard the phrase, "Proper planning prevents poor performance." This is a mantra that OD professionals should learn early in their careers to ensure the success of planned interventions. However, all the energetic planning in the world does not guarantee the successful implementation of a plan. According to Burke (2013) *implementation,* or the launch phase, means the execution of the intervention and is at the heart of any OD project, but it can also be tricky while working within an active organization—much like juggling balls on a moving train. The OD practitioner must be mindful of the basic components—such as data keeping, the intervention itself, and activities oriented toward the maintenance and management of the OD process—to keep all the balls from dropping while the organization continues to function. How these aspects are handled may make or break the change process and rely heavily on the skill and persistence of the OD professional.

Earlier in this book you learned about the importance of assessment and action planning, but the implementation phase may require frequent adjustments to various other phases in different areas of the organization. This phase is dynamic, organic, and very interactive—and it must be initiated from top management. All OD interventions require employee participation and commitment, but the implementation stage requires continuous and sustained support from top management along with the change agent (Cummings and Worley 2014).

Change is not easy, and applying OD interventions is not always a simple, systematic process. It involves constant assessment, communication, and decision making, guided by the ethics of running organizations, respecting people, and managing change (Anderson 2013). Kanter, Stein, and Jick (1992) also remind us that a powerful and capable leader is required for OD interventions: "These change advocates play a critical role in creating a company vision, motivating company employees to embrace that vision, and crafting an organizational structure that consistently rewards those who strive toward the realization of the vision" (384).

In this chapter we examine possible interventions for working with individual, group, organization, and international levels during the implementation phase. Keep this vital stage clear, simple, time-efficient, and valuable, or the ultimate intervention goal, and organizational health, may be lost (Cummings and Worley 2014; Beckhard 1969).

Rothwell et al. (2010) suggest taking six steps during the implementation process:

1. Remember the big picture. OD uses a systems perspective and views organizations as one large system with interacting parts, similar to the human body. When changing one area of the organization, effects could spread to another—much like ripples that spread across the surface of a pool when a stone is dropped into the water. With any system, the whole differs from the individual parts. By shifting focus from the parts to the whole, we can better grasp the connections between the different elements of an organization.

2. Choose the right interventions. It is often said, "If you only have a hammer, every problem looks like a nail." As an OD professional, it is important not only to be familiar with all available tools, but to also research the problem enough to know which intervention will work best for your given situation. It is always best to select interventions that will maximize busy employees' time and accelerate the change process.

3. Use a sound change model to plan and manage the change process. A valid change model should have been built into the project action plan in the planning phase to guide the change process. However, feedback loops are needed to learn what is working and what is not. These may include surveys, interviews, focus groups, key personnel monitoring the change, and so on.

4. Keep people engaged and make the incentive for change greater than the incentive to stay the same. Keeping a change initiative omnipresent is often a challenge for the OD practitioner. People are busy and leadership changes, but keep the change initiative fresh in people's minds. This

can be done by "picking some low hanging fruit," for example making an early win visible to most of the organization, giving positive communication to leaders, or by providing frequent reminders about change goals and purpose. It is also important to keep the incentive to change greater than the incentive to stay the same.

5. Identify and manage resistance to change. Resistance to change is often a natural reaction when people are asked to do something differently. There is usually anxiety and stress about the unknown. However, how an OD practitioner handles this resistance often makes the difference. Natural resistance to change can be reduced by the actions taken and how employees are involved in the change process. Optimally, all employees involved in the change can talk about it and provide input; however, that depends on the size of the initiative. But even a company-wide change effort can be discussed within individual departments to break down resistance and enable conversation about valid concerns.

6. Follow through and learn from the process. Reflection should happen throughout the OD process, concentrating on both what was done and what is left to be done to create and sustain the change. It often takes considerable persistence from the OD professional to follow through with the change initiative, yet few take the time to reflect on and learn from the process.

Many changes require multiple interventions, so a professional OD practitioner should be trained in a few different techniques to be prepared for any situation. Because OD can affect organizations at different levels, interventions should also be targeted toward various levels, depending on the analysis and the expected results of the intervention. However, selecting the proper intervention cannot simply be looked at as change for change's sake, but rather an integrated practice aimed at increasing the overall organizational effectiveness (Cummings and Worley 2014).

Individual-Level Interventions

The globe is shrinking—now more than ever we need to learn to work with various ages, cultures, and belief systems. Today's organizational success is all about developing talented individuals armed with information and trained to lead their organization in the battle of business. Strengthening individual employees benefits the entire organization.

Individual-level interventions aim to improve organizational performance by developing skills among individuals, and keeping the OD initiative on the minds of employees. Given their influence on organizational well-being, individual-level interventions are probably the most widely used by organizations. They concentrate on training and development, recruitment, replacement or displacement, and coaching and mentoring (Burke 2013; Rothwell and Chee 2013).

Coaching and mentoring are two popular individual-level interventions. These two methods use the same skills and approach providing guidance in a person's life, but coaching is short-term and task-based, whereas mentoring creates a longer-term relationship. Focused on issues such as public speaking or project planning, coaching is led by someone capable of assisting the mentee in developing the needed skill. Research shows that coaching provides insight, awareness, focus, and skills, and is now practiced in most parts of the world (Hawkins and Smith 2013). Likewise, mentoring is about building a relationship and may encompass any area affecting the mentee's personal career, such as confidence, self-perception, or balance between work life and home life. Informal mentoring has happened for quite a long time, but the actual science of mentoring is a fairly recent development (Hawkins and Smith 2013). The Chartered Institute of Personnel and Development (CIPD) developed a list of some mentoring and coaching characteristics, which were adapted into Figure 5-1.

Figure 5-1. List of Mentoring and Coaching Characteristics from the Chartered Institute of Personnel and Development

Coaching	Mentoring
Relationship has a set duration	Ongoing relationship
Structured with a specific agenda	Informal facilitation with no set agenda
Short term, focused on achieving specific goals	Long term, with a broader view of career and personal development
Usually a position that comes with the job	Usually selected by the mentee as someone who can pass on his or her knowledge and experience
Task or teamwork focused	Life focused, broad view
Performance focused	Individual growth and learning
Coach is valued because of his or her position within the organization	Mentor is influential because of his or her perceived value to open doors

Adapted from www.cipd.co.uk.

A second group of individual-level interventions comprises methods—including Training Groups (T-Groups), Myers-Briggs Type Indicator, and DiSC—that increase self-awareness. These tools are based off the Johari Window Model (Luft and Ingham 1955), which describes the process of human interaction via a four-paned window (see Figure 5-2).

Since 1955, the Johari Window, often referred to as a disclosure or feedback model of self-awareness, has given us personality insights (Tandon 2013). The four panes split personal awareness into four quadrants: open, blind, hidden, and unknown. The open pane represents "items you and I both know about me"—it could be my name or facts about me. When people first meet, this pane is small. The blind pane represents "items I am not aware of but that you know about me," such as powdered sugar on my face from a donut, or my habit of subconsciously avoiding eye contact. The hidden pane represents "things you do not know but that I know about myself," such as my favorite food or the name of my pet. As we get to know each other, self-disclosure becomes easier and you will learn even more about me and the open pane gets larger. The last pane, unknown, represents "things that neither you nor I know about myself." The unknown pane might include the line, "being shy, I didn't realize it would be so easy to talk to a coworker about my feelings for this Johari Window, and the coworker didn't realize it either." The whole idea is to increase the open area while decreasing the blind area.

Figure 5-2. The Johari Window

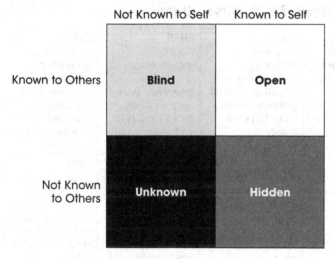

Adapted from Luft and Ingham (1955).

Training Groups, or T-Groups, began at National Training Laboratories Institute in Bethel, Maine, in 1947, and were the basis for current team building techniques (Gallagher 2012). By bringing together a small group of people in a relatively unstructured environment, participants are provided an opportunity to examine their own behavior and learn how to communicate more efficiently in a group.

The Myers-Briggs Type Indicator (MBTI) was first developed by psychologist Carl Jung in 1943, and measures personality types on four quadrants: extroversion and introversion, sensing and intuitive, thinking and feeling, and judging and perceiving (See Figure 5-3; adapted from Myers, Kirby, and Myers 1993). The resulting personality profiles can be used to help explain how people perceive the world around them, and correspondingly to help employers improve employees' performance. The MBTI is an ideal tool for individual development because it shows 16 different personality types, and is extremely straightforward and non-threatening (Abrams 2011).

Figure 5-3. Myers-Briggs Personalities

ESTP	ESFP	ENFP	ENTP
On-the-spot problem solvers, Focus on getting results, Dislike long explanations	Outgoing, Accepting, Friendly, Enjoy everything, Sound common sense, Likes facts not theory	Warmly enthusiastic, Distractible, Ingenious, Does not plan ahead, Rely on ability to improvise	Quick, Good at many things, Stimulating company, Alert, Finds logical reasons for what they want, May argue for fun
ESTJ	**ESFJ**	**ENFJ**	**ENTJ**
Practical, Realistic, Decisive, Matter of fact, Not interested in abstract or theories, Organizer	Warm hearted, talkative, Popular, Conscientious, Need encouragement and praise, Need harmony	Responsible, Responsive, Responds to praise and criticism, Sociable, Popular, Sympathetic	Frank, Decisive, Leaders in activities, Good at reasoning, Enjoy adding to their knowledge, Likes to talk
ISTJ	**ISFJ**	**INFJ**	**INTJ**
Serious, Quiet, Practical, Logical, Matter of fact, Dependable, Realistic, Take responsibility	Quiet, Friendly, Responsible, Thorough, Painstaking conscientious, Accurate, Concerned for Others	Succeed by perseverance, Originality, Quietly forceful, Conscientious, Principles, Concerned for others	Original minds, Great drive, Long range vision, Organized, Skeptical, Critical, Independent, High standards, Determined
ISTP	**ISFP**	**INFP**	**INTP**
Quiet, Reserved, Observing, Mechanical, Cause/Effect, How and why things work, Find practical solutions	Retiring, Quiet, Friendly, Sensitive, Kind, Modest, Shun disagreements, Do not force their opinion	Quiet observers, Idealistic, Loyal, Courteous, Adaptable, Flexible, Little concern for possessions or surroundings	Quiet and reserved, Theoretical, Scientific problem solvers, Logical, No small talk, Sharply defined interests

Adapted from Myers, Kirby, and Myers (1993).

The final personal self-awareness intervention based on the Johari Window is DiSC, which stands for dominance, influence, steadiness, and conscientiousness. Designed by Williams Marston in 1972, this profiling system examines the behavior of yourself and your coworkers by testing word associations to identify 15 patterns. In this way, the individual can gain a better understanding of behavior, temperament, and personality to maximize strengths and minimize weaknesses (Everything DiSC 2010).

An additional individual-level intervention is training and development, which encompasses a wide range of topics to fill gaps in skills or knowledge. Individuals are the main source for corporate innovation, so it is imperative to successfully develop all employees (Sung and Choi 2014). Examples of training and development topics include sales, leadership development, conflict management, computer skills, or public speaking.

Finally, we would be remiss without mentioning the importance of using feedback, or information received about an employee's performance, as a basis for improvement. While working with others in a group or organization, it is important for a person to accept feedback, consider it positively, and then use the information to influence personal growth and decision making (Folkman 2006). A 360-degree feedback is a specific type of feedback, which takes its name from all members of an employee's immediate work circle—such as subordinates, peers, supervisors—performing assessments, as well as a self-evaluation (Edwards and Ewen 1996).

Other areas to examine at the individual level are critical processes, such as job descriptions, policy manuals, and responsibility charting. These areas offer collaboration between the here-and-now of human resources and the vision of the organization development intervention.

Ideally, there should always be a balance between work efficiency and individual job satisfaction.

Case Study: Applying an Individual-Level Intervention

Veronica Grey, a computer operator at Lake Health Services, noticed that her supervisor gave very little positive feedback to her or colleagues that had recently joined the unit. The supervisor was also communicating and delegating work assignments primarily to the senior staff members in the department. As a result, Veronica and her colleagues felt rejected, believing that their contributions were not valued.

After trying to address this issue for more than two years without success, Veronica decided to do something about the situation, and met with two of her colleagues to discuss it. They took the information back to their respective functional areas, and then selected three staff members, of whom Veronica was the spokesperson, and scheduled a meeting with their director, Sonia Patel.

Sonia was already aware of the situation because of anonymous mail she had received from the staff. She tried to intervene on several occasions and recommended training in leadership and communication, which the supervisor attended, thinking that it was routine training for all managers and supervisors. However, Sonia never really sat down with the supervisor to address the specific complaints because productivity was the only important criteria she applied in assessing her staff.

Unfortunately the issue got to a point where Sonia could no longer ignore it, so she called the supervisor in to discuss claims made by the staff. The two had a frank discussion and jointly agreed on a way forward. The first recommendation was a 360-degree performance management assessment, which included Sonia, peers, and some of the employees reporting to the supervisor. The outcome of the assessment highlighted a need for an extended intervention focused on dealing with employee expectations. Sonia used this as a building block for an individual-level intervention emphasizing the encouragement of positive, powerful self-expectations that would translate to the employees. The intervention included the following.

Mentoring

Sonia fostered a mentoring framework where she and another senior supervisor created opportunities for the supervisor to learn new tasks. She also provided new challenges for the supervisor, ensuring that success at each level built on the challenges of the next level. In addition, the supervisor participated in specifically assigned projects and applied the successes of these interventions to her employees.

Coaching

One-on-one coaching with the supervisor was arranged. The coaching focused on improving what the employee did well, rather than on the employee's weaknesses.

Training and Development

A blended training session was designed, which provided developmental opportunities for the supervisor.

Feedback and Reflection

The director frequently reflected on progress by giving positive verbal and written feedback, interacting and communicating consistently with the supervisor, expressing a sincere commitment to the supervisor's success and ongoing development, and encouraging the employee's expectations to ensure sustainable self-improvement.

Group-Level Interventions

Group-level interventions strive to improve group performance, strengthen team or inter-team relationships, and improve the inter-dependency of team members. These may include goal-setting, problem-solving, and role clarification, however, the possibilities are virtually limitless. Like a great orchestra or an award-winning soccer team, individual participants are not nearly as effective as a team whose members demonstrate commitment to the goal and each other. If part of your group-level intervention helps build a group into a team, it would be wise to first review or create a strategic plan for the group to create understanding and commitment.

It should be noted that there must be a proven need for an OD practitioner to include a group-level intervention. Otherwise, performing an inappropriate intervention on a properly functioning team could have the opposite effects as those anticipated by the practitioner. Cummings and Worley (2014) stated that the practitioner should consider the following factors when working with a team intervention: time available for the activity, the team's willingness to examine processes, how long the team has been together, and the team's permanence.

Team building is an obvious group-level intervention. Enhancing group performance can be accomplished by using various approaches, such as ice breakers or games, which help the members get acquainted. But before any intervention can be used, it is important to understand the five stages for any team-building program:

1. Preparation: This stage should explain the purpose of team-building and gain commitment.

2. Start up and data gathering: This stage sets the norm for the work ahead. It encourages employees to be honest about problems, open with planning ideas, and establishes boundaries for issues that may arise.

3. Data analysis and problem solving: It's now time to act on the previous two steps. Team commitments are set for the remainder of the work.

4. Giving feedback: This stage should share information about team members for the team to increase effectiveness.

5. Action planning: All previous stages culminate in the formation of a team action plan to improve performance. Possible actions that can be taken during this stage include:

   • personal improvement plan

   • contract negotiations

   • assignment summary

   • subunit or team plans.

6. Follow up: This stage is a check to ensure that team members did what they were supposed to do and reflect on how the process worked (Rothwell et al. 2010, 333-338).

A radical approach to managing change is the appreciative inquiry (AI) summit. This approach can be applied to any intervention, but commonly combines large group processes with appreciative inquiry to bring about change across a whole system. According to Jim Ludema (2000), "having the whole system in the room also brings an ecological perspective: All the pieces of the puzzle come together in one place and everyone can gain an appreciation for the whole." The AI summit assumes that every group has positive aspects they cannot tap into without the help of an OD practitioner, and has a 4-D cycle process of discovery, dream, design, and destiny, focusing entirely on what is good, valuable, and energizing for the future, rather than problems or what is broken (Watkins and Stavros 2010).

Have you ever been in a meeting where one person talks and everyone else is quiet? We all have, and end up leaving the meeting feeling that it was a waste of our time. A third group-level intervention, called process consultation, encourages total group interaction (Schein 1992). Schein views process consultation as a core philosophy to establish a relationship, rather than just a consulting technique. One common application of this philosophy is to examine how members of a group interact with each other. The OD practitioner observes group verbal and non-verbal interaction and counts the number of interactions each group member demonstrates while the group is meeting. At the end of the session, the practitioner facilitates a discussion with the members about their thoughts on the interaction. This serves as a mirror to the group to assist with future communications (McLean 2006).

Similar to process consultation, meeting facilitation could also be a viable group-level intervention. In this scenario, the facilitator would set the agenda, establish ground rules, and focus the conversation toward the established outcome of consensus. The facilitator has no stake in the decision of the group, and can assign members to take notes, perform follow-ups, and distribute meeting minutes. Over the years, consultants have learned that if people do not buy into interventions like meeting facilitation, implementations will be misunderstood, and most likely fail. It is imperative that the consultant create an environment that is psychologically safe for the participants to plan and solve problems together to expect success (Kaner 2014).

Finally in group level interventions, the team can use brainstorming to get the creative juices flowing during a meeting. Brainstorming helps people think creatively and generate as many ideas as possible about a topic. This topic is usually given to the group members prior to the meeting to give them the opportunity to think about their responses.

Organizational-Level Interventions

In order to survive in an intensely competitive business environment, today's organizations have to seek innovative organization-wide practices that optimize the use of all resources. As a result, organizations are increasingly focused on human capital and organizational management as a source for developing competitive platforms (Roland 2014). Organizational-level interventions, also known as comprehensive interventions, are therefore change catalysts for the entire organization, rather than through individual subgroups. They can involve mergers, outsourcing, and downsizing, or just a basic restructuring of the organization.

A common intervention at the organizational level is survey-guided development. Invented by Rensis Likert, a man widely known for his unique approach to written surveys, the approach intends to collect data at a variety of levels in an organization, give feedback to survey participants, and stimulate an action plan for the issues uncovered in the survey (Rothwell et al. 2010). However, there are caveats to a company-wide survey, such as the need to create appropriate surveys for the intervention. If the survey is too lengthy, the questions do not pinpoint the intervention, or if the questions are not clear, it may be ineffective and a waste of time. A variety of resources are available for creating surveys, which should be reviewed prior to this intervention. One also needs to be aware that the mere act of performing the survey creates an anticipation of change in the organization, even if nothing is done. Employees will anticipate a change; so if it doesn't happen they may be less likely to cooperate with surveys in the future.

Another organizational-level intervention that usually has an immediate and significant impact is called organization design, or organization redesign. Changes in the organization's structure may mean changes in existing procedures and workflows, but no one wants to disrupt the orderly functioning of the organization. However, changing the structure within an organization may create, or recreate, a sense of authority. Simply having the title of CEO or president does not ensure compliance with interventions when there are competing factors and divergent goals. Employees will not follow a title; they follow good decisions (Lai 2014). Before designing and implementing a new organizational structure or any new processes, it is very important to document the current procedure.

Closely related to structural change is the sociotechnical intervention, which involves interactions between people and machines and the changes that occur in human systems when technology is introduced. If one part of the organization is changed, say a new computer system is implemented, it may increase productivity in one area while creating overall dysfunction to the system as a whole. The interdependencies of people and machines should be continually tested because technology is always changing. And since people are far more flexible than machines, employees are often the ones to adapt. For instance, technology makes it possible to outsource to other countries, integrating communications and processes around the world.

Selecting and developing employees to potentially fill positions within the company is called succession planning. Tippins (2002, 252) suggests that key positions for succession planning should be identified and then employees who may be deficient in certain areas should be developed. Without prior planning, organizations are relying on reactive hiring and are taking a risk in the event of a skills shortage. If an organization wants to improve from good to great during the next decade, it needs to put effective succession planning in place (Kalra and Gupta 2014; Rothwell 2010).

While reviewing organizational-level interventions, it would be remiss to not mention process improvement, sometimes called re-engineering interventions. These interventions are performed at the organizational level and involve examining and improving the processes used by the organization, rather than the people. The processes need to align with the ever changing corporate goals and objectives, and some form of measurement that could include benchmarking, LEAN manufacturing, or six sigma. Often these process interventions are requested specifically by organizations, but the OD practitioner should always be able to justify a process intervention with proper analysis, and never be merely an order taker.

LEAN manufacturing is a business model derived from the Japanese manufacturing industry, which has a core philosophy of doing more with less. LEAN methodically eliminates waste while creating products at the greatest efficiency (Holweg 2007). The basic LEAN principles are:
- Focus on giving the customer value.
- Respect and engage people.
- Eliminate waste to improve the value stream.
- Maintain flow.
- Pull through the system.
- Strive for perfection (Liker 2004).

Six sigma is a metrics-based strategy that strives for as close to perfection as possible. It is a very disciplined approach, focused on eliminating the defects in any manufacturing process (Pyzdek and Keller 2009). It utilizes an identical seven-step model as Total Quality Management, but includes various labels, such as a green belt up to black belt, as the employee's expertise improves through the system.

Last, while examining organizational process interventions it is also natural to consider benchmarking, which is used to compare the business processes of one company to another, or to industry standards. Although the concept seems straightforward, benchmarking is easier said than done. As OD practitioners, it is imperative to justify any interventions. Just because company X performed a successful intervention, does not mean that company Y could do an identical intervention with the same results. Every company has its own unique culture and situation, so finding the best practices of another company at best can be considered a launching pad that enables employees to move beyond replication and actually find meaningful change (Golden-Biddle and Team 2013). Although benchmarking often reveals insights, actual implementation should be used with caution, as only the need for an intervention is supported by data.

The most effective change efforts require multiple interventions at multiple levels with a continuous loop. The intervention is part of a cycle that only ends when the desired result is obtained. But an organization that continuously transforms itself by facilitating the learning of its employees is considered a learning organization (Senge et al. 1994). In this way, the learning organization is acting proactively rather than reactively to situations, and has a much better chance of remaining competitive because the entire organization is interconnected.

International Interventions

When people organize they can form lasting change, as witnessed by those involved in communities around the globe—for instance recent events in Ukraine and Egypt, and on a smaller scale, in Native American reservations within the United States and Canada. Any community or nation can use basic OD principles to develop and set policies to improve the life of its citizens by promoting community development, education, health, and safety.

However, OD practitioners must balance the potential benefits and challenges of working in this international marketplace. Although the basic principles of OD remain the same, OD practitioners must determine the proper intervention and the proper cultural context. The approaches are similar whether a multicultural company is located in Europe, the United States, or the Pacific Rim, although all of these markets require different experiences and skills (Kaynak, Fulmer, and Keys 2013). Likewise, a company that is going international requires leaders who are even more flexible, creative, and resilient than their domestic equivalents. A form of multicultural training is always useful for helping people understand one another. This could be as simple as a panel that talks about their cultures and fields questions, or as elaborate as a formal training session. In many multicultural organizations, stories teach lessons and act as powerful directives for behavior. Listening and understanding an organization's frequently told stories gives clues about its culture. And as an OD professional, a story is always a great training tool.

For companies with employees working in multiple countries, virtual team building is another useful intervention. With modern technological advances, there is both an ability and need for virtual teams in order to corral dispersed intellectual capital and access local markets (Caya, Mortensen, and Pinsonneault 2013). While virtual teams may never physically meet, they can remain linked by a shared purpose. When forming a virtual team one should have a plan that includes a shared goal, a plan of communication, and even what language or measures will be used. Research has found that using team-building exercises, establishing shared norms and a clear team structure helps to ensure team success (Sarker et al. 2001, 50). Even a shared knowledge database that all team members can access in a common language and numeric will help communication since all members have identical information.

Case Study: Global OD Initiative at Blue Ivy Fragrance

Blue Ivy Fragrance (BIF) is a successful company operating in the United States with a wide variety of products. As a result of their success in sales, the company is considering expanding into the global market. The corporate culture is very democratic—it is employee friendly and workers are given the opportunity to buy shares in the company. This culture has contributed to high staff retention, high productivity, and a loyal workforce for more than 10 years. However, the board of directors wondered if workers would be provided with similar rights in China, Russia, or India. These countries were chosen based on the size of their population and economies. The board decides to delegate the entire initiative to BIF CEO, Paul Johnson.

You are the OD consultant working for BIF. Paul wants you to be the project manager for this global OD initiative. You have been with the company for more than seven years and have had great success with internal OD interventions. You have theoretical knowledge about global OD initiatives, but very little exposure to China, Russia, or India. In previous research, you also discovered that running an American company within different cultures does not always translate successfully. In fact, new global business initiatives often take a long time to become successful. And most international efforts fail because U.S. management teams are unaware of the context in which they will be operating.

You start thinking about what will be needed to support this intervention. Perhaps with the right people and the right knowledge this global effort could work. You are also very aware that the practice of OD strives to co-create global wisdom and embrace a systemic perspective where people are interrelated—operating under a deep understanding of respect for natural systems, upholding the dynamics of self-organizing and collective consciousness, and ethically serving societies in a sustainable way (Rothwell et al. 2010).

You decide to invite three consultants with global expertise to help brainstorm the effects of this global roll-out and come up with a plan of action. What would you do? Take a few moments to write down some suggestions. If you are in a classroom or group, feel free to discuss possible options with others. When you're ready, take a look at Figure 5-4.

Figure 5-4. A Brief Example of an Action Plan for BIF to Go Global

What	When	Who is Responsible?
• Select a highly qualified team of global OD professionals and local business people representing the regions using a strategic sourcing strategy	January-March	• BIF and global OD consultants
• Appoint a global CEO and a local or international OD consultant per region		
• Subcontract with legal and marketing local expertise		

What	When	Who is Responsible?
• Conduct rigorous research that includes the technical as well as societal, economic, and regulatory aspects of doing business in all three regions	April-June	• OD consultant examines cultural and behavioral tendencies that define consumer habits and employee needs • While the marketing and legal experts review the competitive and legal requirement to do business in these countries
• Analyze and apply research to inform the proceedings	July-September	• Regional OD consultants bring teams together and scenario planning will happen. Creating various possible scenarios of how to go about implementing the business plan.
• Define strategy and criteria for execution of strategy, structure, design, people, processes and procedures, reward systems and other organizational aspects	September-November	• Local teams with BIF OD consultant
• Launch and measure global success by using appropriate financial and non-financial metrics and measurements to keep plans on track	December	• All team members • Regionally and BIF global OD consultants

Project Management in Organization Development

"Today, companies are increasingly implementing change through projects that not only help them thrive but also, very often, enable them to simply survive" (Rahschulte, Herrli, and Herrli 2009, 8). Studies have indicated that approximately 25 percent of organizational change efforts succeed. In 2013, a return on investment (ROI) survey conducted by Towers Watson indicated that, "most change projects fail to meet their objectives. Only 55 percent of the change projects are initially successful, and only one in four are successful in the long run" (6). Although organizational change models have addressed these failures, applying project management principles can further improve the effectiveness of organizational change. The function of a project manager is becoming increasingly important in ensuring that change initiatives are efficiently implemented.

Project management is the discipline of planning, organizing, motivating, and controlling resources to achieve goals that are tied to business objectives. A project is impermanent because it has a beginning and end in time, and therefore a defined scope and resources. Developing a project management system to track what is being done, by whom, and when, is an important step in the process prior to implementing any interventions (McLean 2006). However, it can also be a challenge to achieve every project objective within the predetermined parameters of time, money, and scope.

Traditionally, contemporary project management is directed by top management; hence it is a top-down approach. The project manager hands down all direction to each participant, and the interventions are often influenced by the manager's emotions and opinions (Filev 2008). However, the OD practitioner should not try to manage the project, but instead should act as a third-party change agent, or facilitator, with proactive input from everyone on the team. This bottom-up approach is aligned with the organic OD principles of empowering everyone to be actively involved in the project.

"Project management and change management are two sides of the same coin" (Jarocki 2011, 64) where change management focuses on the soft aspects of change (such as people) and project management focuses on the hard aspects of change (such as tasks). Organization development practitioners must be able to communicate, motivate, resolve conflict, and manage performance. In addition, they must also be able to develop detailed plans, manage time, assess risk, assure quality control, and administer budget constraints. However, the reverse is also true; project managers must be able to simultaneously manage human and organizational change and adopt change models using high-level models and concept. The following sections discuss the project management elements and how they can support any organizational change efforts.

Initiating

The initiating phase involves clarifying the business needs, defining the project, obtaining financial resources, and identifying the external and internal stakeholders of the project. One of the main reasons that change efforts fail is that key stakeholders rarely have a clear understanding of the change's purpose and what is involved. However, the initiation phase emphasizes the importance of understanding the need, ascertaining the purpose, and establishing the goals and deliverables of the change project.

Planning

The planning phase involves determining the total scope of the project, defining and refining project objectives, and developing a course of action to achieve the objectives. This phase considers critical components including time, cost, and other resources that are often the main barriers to a successful change effort. The planning phase is when the task lists, resource plan, communication plan, budget plan, and the initial schedule of the project are created. In addition, this phase identifies the roles and responsibilities of key stakeholders.

Executing

The executing phase involves the processes to complete the work and accomplish the project objectives. These processes help to manage time, cost, and quality. In addition, this phase requires several management concepts, including time management, cost management, quality management, change management, risk management, issue management, procurement management, acceptance management, and communication management.

Monitoring and Controlling

The monitoring and controlling phase involves updating the project plan in conjunction with all other phases. As previously discussed, change is complex, and the outcomes of change are not easily predictable. When any changes are introduced into a system, unforeseen outcomes might impact the viability of the project. Therefore, constant monitoring of time, cost, quality, change, risks, and other issues are important to consider.

Closing

The closing phase involves finalizing all activities to formally complete the project and meet all contractual obligations.

Case Study: Apply the Project Management Phases to plan for an Intervention at Cumberland Valley University

Cumberland Valley University (CVU) is in a key transition period marked by rapid growth in staff and faculty. During the past 10 years, economic growth had stimulated an increase in the number of townhouse complexes in the area and that, combined with a major highway nearby, attracted a growing number of students from nearby metropolitan areas. By 2007, the university had grown substantially—from 5,500 to 12,000 students and from about 500 to 1,700 staff and faculty.

You are an OD practitioner working in higher education and the director of human resources has approached you to discuss a possible OD intervention. At your first meeting, the director provides you with the following background information:

- HR has largely played a compliance role.
- The department has been operating with no strategic plan, although within the confines of the university's strategic priorities.
- The department has been receiving many customer service–related complaints from staff and faculty, such as:
  » a lack of standard procedures for the recruitment process and orientation of newly appointed staff
  » very little collaboration between the functional units, as evidenced by the fact that the same information is repeatedly requested
  » the response time takes forever
  » mistakes are repeatedly being made on paychecks
  » when someone is out of the office that functional area comes to a standstill.

You agree to intervene as an OD consultant and consider using a project management approach. Take a few moments and decide how you would apply the different phases, what you would do, and what project management elements you would focus on to shape your intervention. When you are ready, you can compare Figure 5-5 with your response.

Figure 5-5. Project Management Plan With Elements From the 5 Phases

Project Management Phases	OD Consultant's Responsibilities	Project Management Elements
Initiating	Facilitate discussion sessions with various university directors to gain intervention sponsorship.	• Clarify the business needs with various stakeholder groups, internal and external, concerning this issue. • Create consensus among stakeholder groups. • Look at the university's strategic priorities and what the university would like to achieve with this intervention. • Report back to the VP and president—displaying the need for change and identify broad outcomes. • Provide a workshop on the soft skills of leading change: How to be sensitive to employee needs, display confidence, a sense of importance, and urgency to ensure committed sponsorship.
Planning	Develop or identify an OD change model (see chapter 2) and create alignment.	• Do a formal needs analysis and report back. • Establish a cross-functional team representative of all the stakeholders and develop a code of conduct and ethics. • Introduce appropriate communication and decision-making tools and protocols. • Define the scope of the intervention and resources available. • Estimate the cost of the intervention or find out what budget estimation has been set aside. • Develop an action plan and identity roles and responsibilities. • Brainstorm goals and deliverables, and identify short, medium, and long-term milestones.

Project Management Phases	OD Consultant's Responsibilities	Project Management Elements
Executing	Provide the team with supporting material and create a change champion network among the different directorates.	• Develop an issue-focused database where change champions can input feedback on areas of concern, so alerts can be instantaneously pushed to others in the intervention. • Manage time, cost, and quality of the intervention. • Manage procurement and ensure effective communication. • Manage risk, conflict, and resistance to change and deal with challenges in a timely manner. • Review and reflect on progress continuously. • Celebrate and reward milestones achieved.
Monitoring and Controlling	Update the project plan as necessary and in conjunction with all other phases.	• Consciously monitor the time, cost, quality, change, risks, and other issues of importance. • Mentor and coach individuals where additional support is needed. • Delegate to ensure sustainability of skills for long-term implementation.
Closing	Finalizing all activities.	• Evaluation of the intervention. • Formally complete the project and meet all contractual obligations. • Provide sponsors, the intervention team, and participants with constructive feedback and solid numbers for the scope, cost, and time of the intervention. • Ensure support and follow-up after close out.

Adapted from Jarocki (2011).

In conclusion, this chapter examined possible interventions for working with individuals, groups, organizations, and international global groups during the implementation phase. Many of the fundamentals and key elements involved in planning, implementing, and evaluating were presented. The phases are dynamic, organic, and very interactive—and must be initiated from top management. All OD interventions require employee participation and commitment, but the implementation stage requires continuous and sustained support from top management, as well as the change agent. This may appear time consuming, labor intensive, and overwhelming, but by following a systematic process you will increase the likelihood of success.

Worksheet 5-1. Exercise: Organization Development and Change Implementation

Directions: Respond to the questions concerning every phase of implementation in an OD initiative.		
Phases in Implementing OD and Change Interventions	What Is the Role of the OD Consultant?	What is the Purpose of This Phase?
Phase 1 Launching the Intervention	What will you do to improve your understanding of the intervention and any performance challenges in this phase?	
Phase 2 Structured Interviews	Why will you conduct interviews with key players and what information do you hope to obtain?	
Phase 3 Assessment Report	What types of reports will you compile that indicate the data you have collected and the proposal(s) you will be making?	
Phase 4 Discuss the Organization Assessment Report with the Client	With whom will you discuss the report? List possible issues that you would like to cover.	

Phases in Implementing OD and Change Interventions	What Is the Role of the OD Consultant?	What is the Purpose of This Phase?
Phase 5 Creating Buy-In at the Management Level	How will you create buy-in within the organization?	

Adapted from www.ackerdeboeck.com/organization/organization
-development-exercise.

Additional Reading
Online Links

- An entire table of incredible project management resources can be found at www.niwotridge.com/Resources/PM-SWEResources/PMResources.htm.

- This website includes free templates, webinars, books, and online videos. www.projectmanager.com.

- This website provides more information through whitepapers, books, webinars, and training. www.projectsatwork.com.

- The Project Management Institute guide and standards can be found at www.pmi.org/PMBOK-Guide-and-Standards.aspx.

- An online resource guide to project management can be found at http://quickbase.intuit.com/articles/online-resources-guide-to-project-management.

- This page compares different project management software programs. http://en.wikipedia.org/wiki/Comparison_of_project_management_software.

- This page reviews project management services and features to look out for when shopping for a service. www.projectmanagementsoftware.com.

- This is a technology and project management blog. http://fearnoproject.com.

Project Managing With Google Apps

- Mavenlink.

- Smartsheet.

- Teambox Project Management.

Books

- Horine, G.M. 2005. *Absolute Beginner's Guide to Project Management*. Indianapolis, IN: Que Publishing.

- Kaplan, R.S., and D.P. Norton. 1996. *The Balanced Scorecard: Translating Strategy Into Action*. Cambridge, MA: Harvard Business Review Press.

- Berger, L.A., and M.J. Sikora. 1993. *The Change Management Handbook: A Road Map to Corporate Transformation*. New York: McGraw-Hill.

6

Ethics and Values in Organization Development

Cynthia M. Corn

*"We do not act rightly because we have virtue or excellence, but we rather
have those because we have acted rightly."*
—Aristotle, Greek philosopher

This chapter explores current thought on values and ethics in OD. In
doing so, it:

- looks at what it takes to remain ethical in the field

- explores ethical decision-making, and examines various codes
  of ethics related to OD

- presents models for ethical decision making.

Prominent economist Milton Friedman once said, "There *is* only one
responsibility of business—to use its resources and engage in activities
designed to increase its profits so long as it stays within the rules of the
game" (Zimmerli, Richter, and Holzinger 2007, 173). However, the question then becomes: What are the rules of the game?

The field of organization development is driven by values that may often conflict with those of clients seeking to increase their profits. In this age of ethical scandals, the OD field requires that we take a closer look at our own values and ethics. Through a process of self-examination and reflection, it is possible to develop the ability to continuously think and act ethically.

What Are Values and Ethics?

Values are standards of importance (Rothwell et al. 2010). Consider the word "evaluate." When we evaluate something, we compare it to a given standard. We determine whether it meets that standard, falls short, comes close, or far exceeds. Typical values include honesty, integrity, compassion, courage, honor, responsibility, patriotism, respect, and fairness.

Ethics, on the other hand, are defined as "standards of good/bad or right/wrong behavior based on values" (Rothwell et al. 2010). When we act in ways consistent with our beliefs, we characterize that as acting ethically, whereas unethical behavior goes against our sense of right and wrong. If a society has a single religious or cultural belief system, as some do, it is possible that all members have the same ideas about what is ethical. Conversely, people living in societies without a uniform cultural belief system may not agree on whether a given action is considered ethical or unethical. In other words, determining whether or not a behavior is ethical is both an individual and a societal decision.

It is important to establish your own code of conduct—one that is ethical and minimizes your liabilities as a consultant (McNamara 2006). Create your own mission, vision, and value statements so that when change efforts get chaotic, and they will, you can refer back to your own guidepost for proper behavior.

Clients

As an OD practitioner, you will often have to make difficult decisions. Worley and Feyerherm (2003) examined the values associated with the field of OD and determined that, "OD was founded on humanistic values and ethical concerns like democracy and social justice; it was viewed by some as the organization's conscience. Most practitioners would agree that OD tends to emphasize human development, fairness, openness, choice, and balancing of autonomy and constraint" (99).

However, many feel that this perspective, which is based on human values, is lost to the temptation to do something unethical for financial gain. In every step of the OD process, a practitioner should examine, reflect, and take proactive steps in areas that could turn into ethical dilemmas. Start by determining who the client is—is it the person who paid the bill and signed the contract, or the person to whom you are giving information? What is the client's perception of the project—is it the same as yours? And most importantly, if you initially spoke to a gatekeeper and not the CEO, is upper management on board with the change effort, and is it in line with their organizational vision, mission, and values?

You may also run into the dilemma of not agreeing with the location, business products, or business practices of a potential client. For instance, a member of PETA (People for the Ethical Treatment of Animals) may not ethically agree to contract with a pharmaceutical company that performs animal testing. If the practitioner has any moral issues that could cloud objectivity, he or she should avoid working with that organization.

Asking a few ethical questions may assist the consultant in really getting to know the client. Consultants could ask questions such as:
  • What is the core purpose of the company other than profit?

- What are the corporate core values?
- What are the company's short and long term goals?

At that stage, the consultant can determine whether he can ethically agree to contract with the company or not.

The OD Process

It is possible that the OD practitioner and the client will have different goals, values, needs, skills, and abilities. It is important to address these differences to prevent subsequent interventions from resulting in conflict or ambiguity. Isolating these ethical dilemmas at various stages of the OD process requires constant examination and reflection of the relationship between the OD practitioner and the client, and how that relationship changes throughout the intervention. Figure 6-1, a process relational model of organization development, is a visual representation of the 10 stages of OD.

Figure 6-1. A Process Relational Model of Organization Development

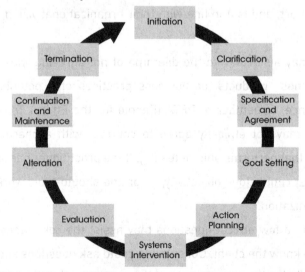

Source: White and Wooten (1983)

On the other hand, if conflict or ambiguity were not addressed at various stages of the OD process, it could result in different types of ethical dilemmas as described by White and Wooten (1983):

- Misrepresentation: Occurs when an OD practitioner promises results that are unreasonable for the intervention, or the client portrays inaccurate expectations and goals. Misrepresentation usually occurs during the entering and contracting phases of the intervention. To prevent misinterpretation, OD practitioners need to establish clear intervention goals with the client.

- Misuse of data: Occurs when data gathered during the entry and diagnostic phases of the OD process is used punitively, usually as a show of power by either the client or consultant. The best way to avoid misuse of data is for the practitioner and client to reach an agreement about how collected data will be stored and used.

- Coercion: Occurs when employees are forced to participate in an OD intervention. That's why it is imperative for the change process to be as transparent and open as possible, with the free consent of the participants.

- Collusion: An improper secret agreement between two or more parties to defraud or deprive others. A good example of collusion in the OD process would be if the OD practitioner and the CEO decide to schedule training when an unpopular manager is on vacation.

- Promising unrealistic outcomes: This is unethical and can reduce the credibility of the OD practitioner.

- Deception and conflict of values: Occurs when the proposed intervention is not clear, or when the OD practitioner and the client don't agree on the goal. At this stage, it is usually prudent for the OD practitioner to withhold services from a company that does not agree with his values.

- Professional or technical ineptness: Occurs when an OD practitioner attempts an intervention in which she has no experience. It is imperative to diagnose the organization and to select an intervention that matches the OD practitioner's own values, skills, and abilities.

Figure 6-2 incorporates 31 potential dilemmas at various stages of the OD process. This is an excellent reference for the OD practitioner, as the nature of the relationship between the practitioner and client changes during the various stages of the process. Please note that implicit in the various dilemmas is the notion that they may be produced by either the practitioner or the client.

Figure 6-2. Organization Development Change Stages, Appropriate Role Behaviors, and Possible Ethical Dilemmas

Stage	Purpose	Role of Consultant	Role of Client System	Dilemmas
Initiation	First Information Sharing	To provide information on background, expertise and experience	To provide information on possible needs, relevant problems, interest of management and representative groups	Misrepresentation of the consultant's skill base and background Misrepresentation of organizational interest
Clarification	Further elaboration of initiation stage	To provide details of education, licensure, operative-values, optimum working conditions	To provide a detailed history of special problems, personnel, marketplace, internal culture, and organizational politics	Inappropriate determination of the client Avoidance of reality testing Inappropriate determination of value orientation

Stage	Purpose	Role of Consultant	Role of Client System	Dilemmas
Specification/ Agreement	Sufficient elaboration of needs, interest, fees, services, working conditions, arrangements	To specify actual services, fees to be charged, timeframe, actual work conditions	To specify whose needs are to be addressed, objectives, and possible evaluative criteria or end-state outcomes	Inappropriate structuring of the goals of the relationship Inappropriate definition of change problem Collusion to exclude outside parties
Diagnosis	To obtain an unfiltered and undistorted view of the organization's problems and processes pinpointing change targets and criterion	To collect data concerning organizational problems and processes and to provide feedback	To assist consultant in data collection	Avoidance of problems Misuse of data Distortion and deletion of data Ownership of data Involuntary consent Confidentiality
Goal Setting/ Action Planning	To establish the specific goals and strategies to be used	To agree mutually with the client system on the goals and strategies to be used	To agree mutually with the consultant on the goals and strategies to be used	Inappropriate choice of intervention goal and targets Inappropriate choice of operative means

Stage	Purpose	Role of Consultant	Role of Client System	Dilemmas
Systems Intervention	The intervention into ongoing behaviors, structures, and processes	To intervene at specific targets, at a specific depth	To invest the energy and resources required by planned intervention	Assimilation into culture Inappropriate depth of intervention Coercion vs. choice, freedom, and consent to participate Environmental manipulation
Evaluation	To determine the effectiveness of the intervention strategies, energy, and resources used, as well as the consultant-client system relationship	To gather data on specified targets and report findings to the client system	To analyze the evaluation data and determine effectiveness of the intervention	Misuse of data Deletion and distortion of data
Alteration	To modify change strategies, depth, level, targets, or resources, utilized if necessary	To make alteration to meet original goals, or to develop new mutual goals and strategies with client system	To make known needs and expectations, and to provide the context for a modification of the original agreement, if necessary	Failure to change and lack goals, of flexibility Adoption of inappropriate strategy

Stage	Purpose	Role of Consultant	Role of Client System	Dilemmas
Continuation/ Maintenance	To monitor and maintain ongoing strategies, provide periodic checks, continue intervention based on original or altered plans and strategies	To specify the parameters of the continuation and the maintenance of relationship	To provide or allocate the resources required to maintain or continue the intervention	Inappropriate reduction of dependency Redundancy of effort Withholding of services
Termination	To have the consultant disenfranchise self from the client system and establish a long-term monitoring system	To fulfill the role agreed on in previous stages and evaluate overall effectiveness from feedback from the client system	To determine the organization's state of health and whether it has developed the adaptive change process	Inappropriate transition of change effort to internal sources Premature exit Failure to monitor change

Source: White and Wooten (1983).

Obviously there are many important points to think about when starting a project, but in the end all these answers will help clarify your role within the project and avoid potential ethical dilemmas from the start.

Information

Once both the project scope and client expectations are clearly established, it is important to determine what happens to the information gathered during the intervention to avoid any misuse of data. The words *confidential* and *anonymous* are often confused when discussing information or data obtained during an OD intervention. Confidential means that information cannot be shared at all, whereas anonymous means that the information can be shared, but the source of the information cannot (McLean 2006).

It is imperative that the OD practitioner safeguards the information gathered during the intervention, but it is also important to determine how that information will be used, how it will be disseminated, and to whom. If your project scope and contract determine one goal, but the client is using your information for another, perhaps selfish goal, that is an ethical dilemma. If the board of directors—which is not your client, but is paying the consulting bill—requests data gathered during the project, what would you do? Since consultants sometimes work in one industry (manufacturing, for example) they have data that a competitor would be very interested in obtaining. What if a corporate competitor of the company for which you are working contacts you for information? Often a consultant is required to sign a non-compete clause to avoid such a dilemma, or she may be required to refrain from working with competitors for a specific period of time. Ultimately, once the information is gathered and turned over to the client, it should only be used for its original intent.

Likewise, if the OD practitioner learns of information that may be financially profitable to him while working for a particular company, he is prohibited from using that information for his own gain—such as buying the company stock to make a profit, or telling a competitor about a new product.

Money

Billing for OD interventions is done quite differently depending on the practitioner, the location, and the job. Many jobs are billed in a lump sum by estimating the number of hours the intervention will take, while others are billed by the hour. The contract should specifically spell out what work will be done, the fee, how the consultant will be paid and in what time parameter, whether travel time and expenses are paid, how hours working from home are calculated, and if the consultant will be paid by the hour, half-day, or day. Getting this information in writing prior to the intervention makes payment practices clear to the client and avoids the appearance of billing for time not worked. Practitioners often adjust their fees according to the client's budget, and will often do free or pro bono work for the good of the profession.

Sometimes an unexpected development occurs in a project that is beyond the area of expertise of the contracted practitioner. In this case, the client is usually referred to another consultant. But who calls in the second consultant—you or the company for which you are working? Does the additional practitioner work for you or the company? And who will pay her? In addition, does the initial contracted practitioner require a quid pro quo or monetary tip for making the recommendation? These questions need to be considered before the additional practitioner begins work.

It should also be noted that not every country holds the same views toward giving and receiving gifts and payments. In the United States, this practice (bribery) is illegal. If you are a practitioner working outside your host country, it is important to thoroughly research this practice prior to accepting the contract, otherwise it may be very difficult to determine whether your host organization is offering you a gift or a bribe. In many countries a small gift may be perfectly acceptable, but a large bribe is not. You need to tap into individual value systems to determine what is appropriate, as well as be aware that accepting a bribe may ruin your reputation.

People

While working for an organization, OD practitioners are obliged to follow the same policies required of that organization's employees, regarding sexual harassment and sexual relationships. The OD practitioner must be an objective third party to the organization, and unethical behavior or office romances impinge on the effectiveness of their role. This could also include friendships between the consultant and employees, including things such as playing basketball at lunch with accounting, or going to dinner with the sales department. It's best to stay impartial in order to view the culture objectively and stay focused on the task at hand.

It is also important to remember that each company's culture is unique. This means that an intervention that worked for one organization may not always work for another. It is considered unethical for an OD practitioner to simply plug-and-play a potential solution without proper analysis of the cultural and organizational requirements.

What if the organization requests the implementation of a particular intervention, such as a team-building workshop or seminar on diversity? Has an analysis been performed to justify the outcome of that intervention? Will implementing only the requested intervention without a full-scale analysis truly help or will additional issues arise? In OD, the practitioner should retain a top-to-bottom systems perspective of an organization, similar to a clinical psychologist who continues to ask questions of the client until the latter comes up with the solution themselves. Clients often have the solutions, but they do not always know how to logically get there—that role is played by the OD practitioner.

Another common ethical issue for OD practitioners is a refusal to (or delay in) the skills transferal to the client. The consultant's time with the client is limited and usually contracted, which means that a training timeline should be written into the contract to assure that the necessary skills are transferred to the client prior to separation. Consultants who seek to obtain more hours or an additional contract by delaying this phase, lessen commitment to the profession and are ethically questionable. Likewise, mining for additional projects to extend time with the client and delay separation is most likely unethical.

Code of Ethics

A code of ethics is a statement that has been approved by a professional organization to guide its members' perception of the difference between right and wrong and the application of that understanding to their decisions (McLean 2006). The code of ethics from the International Organization Development Institute is a very helpful guideline, and is provided in the appendix. These codes set the stage for ethical practices, but their true value comes from the frequent discussions that take place between OD practitioners about how to view the intersections between their own values and the OD practices in a global professional community.

Unethical Behavior

Ethics is very subjective and dependent on culture as well as individual and societal decisions. Western cultures value individualism and competition, whereas other cultures value patience and camaraderie (McNamara 2006). Because there are no universal rules in OD consulting, not everyone will agree. Even common industry practices may not always be ethical. However, having strong moral principles is paramount if you would like to continue consulting. Are there ethical dilemmas in which you have been involved or heard about from a colleague? Would you do things differently if you had them to do again? You may even consider discussing ethical dilemmas with other consultants, while obviously protecting the confidentiality of your client. A seasoned consultant often runs into similar situations and can give sage advice to help you find alternative solutions. As discussed earlier in the chapter, organization development was founded on humanistic values and it is still very much a collaborative discipline, with a colleague just a phone call away willing to assist.

In the wake of recent corporate scandals where executives were actually charged for unethical behavior, we are reminded of the need for a deep-rooted culture of integrity. OD practitioners should not need to refer to the law or consult an attorney to know what is right or wrong—it should be part of their vision, mission, and values. If consultants are always acting ethically and professionally, they are ready when confronted with unethical or illegal behavior.

The indictment of insider trading by SAC Capital Advisors and the bribery scandal at GlaxoSmithKline are just two recent cases. SAC bragged about having a "strong culture of compliance," yet it now faces one of the largest insider trading charges in the hedge fund industry, and Glaxo recently admitted to a $450 million bribery scheme (Getnick 2013).

Kenneth Lay and Enron's downfall was one of the most shocking ethics violations of all time. It bankrupted the company, sent several members of its leadership group to prison, and destroyed Arthur Andersen, one of the largest audit firms in the world. Manipulating accounting rules and masking the company's enormous losses and liabilities were just some of the charges. The scandal at Enron resulted in Congress passing the Sarbanes-Oxley Act to improve corporate accountability (Mohr 2013).

More than ever, the health of an organization depends on its ability to adapt to fast-changing events. The challenges facing today's organizations are often global, increasing the demand for OD practitioners and shining a spotlight on the ethical issues surrounding the field.

Additional Reading

While more recent discussions can be found, the classic discussions of organization development values and ethics can be found in the following:

- Gellermann, W., M.S. Frankel, and R.F. Landenson. 1990. *Values and Ethics in Organization and Human Systems Development*. San Francisco: Jossey-Bass.

- Frankel, M.S. 1987. *Values and Ethics in Organization and Human Systems Development: An Annotated Bibliography*. Washington, DC: AAAS Publications.

- White, L.P., and K.C. Wooten. 1996. *Professional Ethics and Practice in Organization Development*. New York: Praeger Publishers.

7
Special Issues in Organization Development

Catherine Haynes

"Complex organizations have to innovate or die, and in so doing they tend to operate at the edge of chaos."
—Burnes (2004)

This chapter offers a practical view of OD information that can be useful in any organization. It discusses special issues in OD, including:

- complexity theory
- technology in OD (group decision support systems)
- sociotechnical systems.

Complexity Theory

Complexity theory (CT) has several other references, particularly in the fields of strategic management and organizational studies. The basic premise is that organizations are treated as a collection of strategies and structures. The interest of early scholars in this theory included such themes as decomposable systems, computational complexity, and the contrast between organic and mechanistic structures.

Complexity theory replaced some of the older organizational theories as noted by Grobman (2005) and Burnes (2004). Scholars were interested in understanding how the scientific concepts of chaos theory, emergence, and complexity could be used to comprehend the complex strategies of organizations. It is important for OD practitioners— whether they are internal or external to the organization—to understand the concepts of CT, which will then give them the leverage they need to be successful in any organization. One way to show this is to think of the organization as a nonlinear natural phenomenon similar to nature. Complex organizations must find ways to survive in a volatile economy; being too stable or unstable can be devastating. Everyone in the organization, including the OD practitioner, must do her part to ensure survival. In nature, for example, too little water will kill some plants, while too much water will kill others. Equilibrium is key, and nature's complex ecosystems must adapt to survive. Organizations must also find equilibrium—complex organizations have to innovate or die, and in so doing they tend to operate at the edge of chaos (Burnes 2004).

Academics and practitioners view organizations through the complexity theory lens, which covers many different disciplines in the natural sciences. Meteorologists, chemists, and biologists all attempt to make mathematical models of the systems in nature. The use of the single word "theory" is not sufficient in explaining this series of complex systems that are consistently changing and in a state of expansion in some areas, while reducing in others. Thus researchers, such as Waclawski, Church, and Burke (1995), use the term theories to explain such changing phenomena. Some events that create chaos include a new CEO, employee movements and high turnover, and volatility in the marketplace. These events could represent either posi-tive or negative changes within the organization. While a change may be positive for some, it can be negative for others. For example, new hires can be viewed positively as organization growth; however if the new hires were necessary due to high employee turnover, that can be viewed negatively, thus contributing to more chaos.

Burnes (2005) contended that complexity theories should be used as metaphors to help us gain insights into organizations. In so doing we are able to test the values of those insights. While some organizations have been around for many years, other have come and gone. What makes the long-standing organization successful? Organizations are complex systems that are constantly changing per Brown and Eisenhardt (1997). Are the old organizations adapting to the complexity of modern-day busi-ness? If that is the case, the new ones should not fail. Complex organiza-tions should always be learning from their past, reinventing themselves in the present, and preparing for the future.

Changes in the organization could include the creation of new auto-mated systems, such as computers to assist employees in completing work and in some instances to replace employees who complete routine tasks. For example, some employees were hired by a mail organi-zation to do heavy lifting and to sort boxes and small parcels. Over a period of time, the organization "lost" many of these employees (mostly men) due to back and neck injuries. Still, there were other employees eager to replace the injured workers. Eventually the organization made changes to its operations by automating the heavy lifting—robots were now completing the tasks that caused many workers' injuries. The orga-nization then retrained some of the workers as technicians, program-mers, and maintenance personnel for the robots. During the transition between human (manual) and machine (mechanical) this organization was is a steady state of chaos, however in order for the organization survive it needed to operate on the edge of chaos and be able to change (Burnes 2004).

There are many complex reasons why some organizations are not successful. Some do not make it through such events as a new CEO, gossip in the news, new product innovations, or the loss of employees with organizational knowledge. Other organizations make it through what seem like similar or even worse events. Why? How can understanding complexity theory help an OD practitioner? An OD practitioner understands that organizations are complex structures with many moving parts and variations, where one area can be successful and others need more work. Internal consultants should know the inner workings of their particular organization, while external practitioners understand how organizations should operate in general terms.

To be successful organizations must change with the times—they can't survive solely on past successes.

Technology Use in OD (Group Decision Support Systems)

Is change a phenomenon of time? If so, how does that manifest in the use of technology in OD? With the days of brainstorming on paper becoming shorter and shorter and the landscape of OD continuously changing, it is more important than ever for organizations to embrace technology. Group decision support systems, especially at the upper management levels, are especially important. Associated with collaboration software, the name may change slightly based on who manufactures the product, but the premise and end results are amazing. One example is sociotechnical systems (STS), which is discussed later in this chapter.

Group Decision Support Systems

With the ever-present demand for increasing shareholder profits and decreasing expenses, the use of computer-aided, group-decision-making products is on the rise. Group decision support systems (GDSS) and electronic meeting systems, most commonly referred to as group systems, are web- or electronically based collaboration technologies that combine computing, communication, and decision-support technology into one solution. The system, which can be used across many types of businesses, is best used to help resolve unstructured group problems (Aiken, Vanjani, and Krosp 1995). The GDSS transformed the concept of meetings by offering clients a viable alternative to the traditional setting (Aiken et al. 1995). Today, access to such systems is even more common, thus making face-to-face meetings less costly. The data-driven system allows users to work simultaneously and collaboratively while using the same computer software, shifting the decision-making steps from paper to computer. The group, with the help of a facilitator, decides when one step has been exhausted and it's time to move to the next, thus enhancing productivity. However, the OD practitioner must also keep in mind that not all decisions should be made by a group. Software of this kind can be used synchronously or asynchronously and, if web-based, is not bound by geographical limitations.

Advantages and Disadvantages of Group Decision Support Systems (GDSS)

There are some real advantages to using group decision support systems:

- the ability for the decision makers to be in the same place at the same time
- provides anonymity and the freedom to express ideas (Aiken et al. 1995)

- allows parallel communication (Aiken et al. 1995)
- encourages team building
- inspires better group synergy
- reduces group think
- encourages greater group buy-in to the final decision
- facilitates open communication between employees
- provides immediate feedback
- produces a written report of the final decisions
- promotes group involvement
- keeps group members focused on the task at hand
- allows the group to see everyone's answers and comments.

The disadvantages of using group decision support systems include:

- needs an initial start-up cost
- not appropriate for some decisions
- may lead to loss of the verbal participant
- slow communication—all answers are typed
- requires a facilitator or person skilled in running meetings
- lack of media richness
- less traditional group dynamics
- reduces the social interaction between employees (Aiken et al. 1995).

Researchers have reported that web support systems for group collaborative decision-making provide a structured method of problem identification and ultimate recommendations for solutions or change (Rigopoulos, Psarras, and Askounis 2008). Using the web-based technology of group decision support systems, with the aid of a facilitator and some software adjustments, the application can provide a structured way to solve problems in business surroundings, including human resources and production (Rigopoulos et al. 2008).

Humans Versus Computers and Technology

Outsourcing employees to another country has become common. However, more customers are complaining about poor customer service, and employers are complaining that they cannot find qualified applicants in all locales. This leads to the question: Where are they looking? Are organizations hiring the right people for the jobs and at the right time?

Sociotechnical Systems (STS) is the effective blending of the technical and social systems in an organization. Can humans and technology co-exist effectively in the same organization? It depends. Some believe that no one will ever trust a computer because it would house personal and damaging information that could get in the hands of the wrong person and cause irreparable damage to an organization. However, computers are now used for employee development, training, financial assistance, employee evaluations, and customer service, just to name a few items. Today, employees can work from their personal computer at the office, at home, or anywhere they have access to the Internet. With all that being said, a computer cannot replicate great employee relations or customer service.

Global markets and new technologies are changing the way organizations do business. Mumford (2000) looked at problem-solving activity and uncovered a need for clear guidelines on who does what as far as obtaining technical assistance via either an automated or human system. Humans and technologies can be integrated in ways never seen before. For example, HR managers would forego some current HR functions that can be handled via computer, some which should be automated as much as possible. The OD practitioner should provide guidance or recommendations to organizations that lead to more beneficial uses of human time.

Sociotechnical Systems

The sociotechnical system (STS) in organization development is a complex, multi-layered approach to a theory that allows for interaction between people and technology in the workplace. This can include the transportation of people, cargo, and technologies between destinations. Sociotechnical systems also affect interactions between society's complex organizations and human behavior. The multifaceted organizational interactions between infrastructures and people are well known (Fox 1995). Likewise, Haavik (2011) wrote that there are different approaches to sociotechnical systems, because of the complex aspects of humans, organizations, and technology. Strauch (2010) wrote that sociotechnical systems have a cultural component that can affect operations, and that component must be understood. No one system is the best fit for everyone or every organization.

Careful consideration must be given to each of these areas. Just as an organization must give careful consideration to hiring the right individual for a position, so too must consideration be given when choosing the right technology. Neither one should be cookie-cut; they should be customizable and adjustable to fit the organization. And when a conflict arises, the organization must find a way to handle it. The OD practitioner may be called upon to help find solutions to integrate technology and how humans work together and with technology to achieve work results. Conflicts have negative impacts on individual and team performance. OD practitioners must know their role in an organization and have clear expectations. This role is even more critical for an external consultant due to the organization's expectations and need for measurable and attainable goals and results.

Team-building and team-related issues continue to be areas of major emphasis for the practitioner (Piotrowski and Armstrong 2004). Internal and external OD practitioners influence management and leadership principles used in an organization, as well as changes in actual manager behavior and various training programs in managerial and leadership development contexts. The OD practitioner has several tools, such as organizational assessment and diagnosis, problem-solving sessions, and quality of work-life activities. The practitioner can also add the humanistic values of empowerment and continuous learning to create a holistic change program for the organization (Waclawski et al. 1995).

In his report on cultural factors and their influence on sociotechnical systems operations, Strauch (2010) reported that cultural differences can change the way people interact within the system. Two different skill sets are in effect here: technical and social (Ghosh and Sahney 2011). Culture in this instance refers to both the individual and the organization. For example, organizations employ a variety of individuals from various backgrounds. These individuals must operate and be productive within the organization's culture. Sometimes there are conflicts or cogitative dissonances between the organization and individual culture.

Researchers have argued that changes in an organization occur because someone failed in the past—thus the change occurs to right a wrong. But where did that change originate? The change model process, as mentioned in chapter 2 of this volume, indicates that the process can be managed electronically at the upper management level and have cross-organization implications. The OD practitioner can then be the change agent. In some organizations, it is not unusual for an employee to leave a meeting with more actions than she can reasonably complete, because the organization brought a large number of immediate action items to the table, without leaving enough time for resolution (Weick and Quinn 1999).

Today, forward-thinking CEOs have the edge over those doing business the same old way. There are better ways to handle the immediate actions on the agenda. One such way is through group decision support systems. Another option is sociotechnical systems, which is not just one item, like an operating system, instead they often involve complex networks of systems working together with people and technology to achieve particular goals. For example, some organizations have one desk per employee, while in others one desk may be used by two employees, one on each shift. Both workers are productive while sharing the same workspace. Another example has to do with whole tasks where one employee is responsible for a particular task from beginning to end.

8

The Future of Organization Development

Catherine Haynes

This chapter discusses future trends in OD, including:

- work trends
- self-directed teams
- self-managed teams
- whole systems transformational change
- globalization.

Although no one can predict the future, we can speculate, make reasonable assumptions, and most of all make informed assessments about the future. Should we look at the past to predict the future? Yes, we should. Predictions are commonplace in the stock market and real estate, but they should be just as common in OD, which can be as volatile, with people moving from one organization to the other for many reasons.

As OD practitioners can we predict how or why employees leave? As we discuss the future of OD, two questions come to mind: Where is the OD field going, and what will it look like five or 10 years from now?

Weighing the factors that measure success in the OD field can help minimize the uncertainty. Interest will continue to revolve around making OD more positive (appreciative inquiry), future OD competencies are being discussed and identified, and practitioners are grappling with how humans and technology can effectively work together to achieve results (sociotechnical systems) and engage in whole systems transformations.

In this final chapter it is important to make bold predictions and offer insights on where the field is heading based on research and experience. For OD practitioners, being able to provide the right service at the right time is paramount. OD has immense potential for influencing other HR functions because organizations rely on internal and external OD practitioners for the guidance needed to keep moving forward. Thus, a forward-thinking OD practitioner is a great value-add to any organization. All in all, the OD field gets better and stronger as research provides results that inform the field. A successful OD practitioner must be able to see around the corner in at least these three areas: work trends, globalization, and technology. In 2003 some practitioners predicted that the future of OD was about the alignment of strategy, processes, technology, and people, along with the basic views of how organizations function (Uhlfelder 2003). That same year others predicted that OD practitioners must have a strong cultural presence to be the face of humanism in the organization. Take a minute to think about your own predictions for the future of OD. Use Worksheet 8-1 to record your opinions based on your experiences.

Worksheet 8-1. Predictions About the Future of OD

Directions: Use this tool to record your predictions about the future of OD as you see it. Your predictions will be based on your own personal opinions and lived experiences. When you finish, circulate this activity with others to see what the group predicts. Then discuss the results with everyone in the group and ask the question: What should each person in the group do to prepare for the future?

Your Predictions

Group Predictions

Discussion Points

1. Were your predictions close to those cited by the group?

2. Were there any surprises in your predictions compared to those of the group?

3. Were you surprised by any other predictions?

The OD field crosses international and cultural borders. Although research and writing in OD has experienced a transformation during the past decade, researchers recognized that processes, time, and context play a large part in the generalization of outcomes in research. This makes the future of the field unique and exciting as it moves into the next decade. It is this quest for understanding that led researchers to agree that there should be a deeper and wider engagement or partnership between researchers and practitioners to assist in the funding, production, and dissemination of knowledge within the OD field (Pettigrew, Woodman, and Cameron 2001).

Team Development Process

Why is the team development process still being talked about today, more than 50 years from its inception? The processes of human interaction have not changed. The team development process is an integral part of self-directed and self-managed teams. Human interactions have been studied time and time again. In order to be successful it is important to understand how teams are formed and thus be able to manage expectations from the onset. The organization must be prepared to create successful work teams. Several different personality trait instruments may be used, although they are not intended to be used alone. Instead these instruments should be used in conjunction with competencies to create a complete picture prior to creating the teams. This will provide team members with better self-awareness and better prepare them for working within a group.

Self-Directed Teams

Self-directed work teams represent a paradigm shift from hierarchical top-down management approaches to groups of five to 15 members who work interdependently on tasks. Team members are responsible for managing and performing most aspects of assigned tasks. Douglas et al. (2006) conducted research on one manufacturing firm's transition from a bureaucratic management system to self-directed work teams. As an organization transitions from its original way of doing business to work teams, it does so using its current employees. Communication is essential between members of the new self-directed teams, because the teams are fully responsible for their work and are held accountable for the outcomes.

Similarly, Pettigrew et al. (2001) wrote that communication is an integral part of the organizational switch to include self-directed work groups as part of their management goals. This change also bears on team members' and team leaders' acceptance of the fact that they are now decision makers for the organization.

Many organizations chose to create self-directed teams, which are composed of employees who collaborate to produce a product or service (Beckham 1998). By bringing together individuals with diverse backgrounds, talent levels, experiences, and abilities, self-directed work teams can govern themselves without an external manager—rather, the team leader is selected from within that team. In addition, the team has a great level of influence on what task it does, how it does it, and why it chooses that particular task. In the future, more work will be performed in virtual self-directed work teams, perhaps in collaboration with Artificial Intelligence applications.

Self-Managed Work Teams

High performing self-managed work teams of three to five members can be very successful. Team members must set clear, realistic, and measurable goals based on individual skills and specialized training.

Leadership in self-managed work teams is group focused. There are several advantages of using this approach, especially the fact that the leader is chosen by the team. Another advantage is that the team can solve its own internal conflicts and is responsible for project outcomes. Self-managed work teams are best suited for specific projects, and an organization can save valuable resources by using this approach. It also allows for collaboration between workers from different departments. However, this concept can result in a change in the organizational culture, so it is important to keep the organizational environment in mind.

Project managers, HR practitioners, and management must give careful consideration to individual strengths and abilities prior to placing them on a team. The members of a team depend largely upon the function and desired outcomes. The team's mission (deliverables) must be clear. Teams meet for this purpose only—at the end of the project the team is dispersed.

Opportunities are created when members leave their assigned positions to participate in a work team that creates a temporary void that other employees can be cross-trained to fill (Yeatts and Hyten 1998). The very nature of self-managing teams may lead to more powerful members exercising their power over the team, which can lead to employees who do not want to participate in the team concept. One could argue that self-managing work teams can be a benefit or a hindrance to an organization (Manz 1992), but they are still important for organizational survival in this global economy.

Whole System Transformational Change

Whole systems transformational change (WSTC) is another method of organization development. It is a traumatic, drastic, and often chaotic approach to organizational change that requires a shift in beliefs, attitudes, and cultural values. The WSTC process can facilitate large-scale change efforts (Rothwell 2005). The idea behind it is that once all the organization's decision makers are involved in the event, they can agree on the course of action right then and there, with no need to wait for approval or additional input from the boss.

The success of WSTC requires the entire organization to be self-aware, involved, and on board, not just one team, section, or department. According to Chapman (2002), it is generally used to target formal structures of the organization, prepare employees for doing more, or to lift standards of performance.

To facilitate WSTC, Dubois and Rothwell (2004) indicated that senior executives, HR practitioners, operating managers, and workers must buy-in to the transformation effort. One method for inspiring this ownership of the change is to create a whole systems transformation conference that involves everyone participating in the transformation effort. The participants would assist in facilitating organizational transformation through a series of activities and clear conference objectives. At the end of the conference, a final report would be completed on final outcomes for the entire organization.

Globalization

Organizations must maintain their competitive advantage for success. Is the organization ready to stay ahead of its competitors? Here are some organization strategies to help organizations succeed in a growing global market.

Stay Competitive

In a global marketplace it is imperative for companies to maintain their competitive edge by having a flexible workforce that can adjust to market changes while striving to increase market share. The use of self-managed work teams can be a positive step in that direction and help organizations meet the challenges of global competition (Muthusamy, Wheeler, and Simmons 2005).

Have Reliable Products or Services

To maintain market share, companies must make sure that their products and services are reliable. The company must be willing to implement and modify products or services as research reveals new methods for improvement.

Implement New Processes

Companies can use web-based programs that would allow employees to work from home. This process is beneficial for the organization, the individual, and ultimately the environment with fewer cars on the road.

Support Current Employees

Organizations should be flexible with the work hours and location for employees who are not directly involved with the production process. This includes flexible hours for those who can add value to the organization by working off-hours to maintain customer support while improving internal processes. Some employees can work from home or satellite offices—situations that will enable them to meet company goals while reducing their travel time.

Future Strategies for Individuals

Organizations must maintain their competitive advantage to ensure continued success, and employees must contribute to the overall success of the organization. In some cases the individual must also contribute to a team. A well-rounded individual's contribution to any team is beyond job competencies. As an individual, how prepared are you to meet organizational goals? As an OD practitioner, how prepared are you for the future of OD? Here are some questions for self reflection.

- Have you ever taken a personality inventory? Are you aware of the affect your personality has on others? You are probably aware of your reaction when someone walks into the room, but are you aware of what happens when you walk in?

- Are you up-to-date on industry trends? Some people listen to the sporting news or talk radio so that they can have a conversation with their fellow workers. You can read and stay abreast of improvements in your industry.

- Have you learned anything new about your profession? Make room for self-improvement or individual development. Learn the newest advances in your field. This may include attending a class or going to a seminar or conference.

- Do you know the company's strategic plan? One benefit of having this information is being able to plan ahead or grow with the company.

- Are you an organizational bystander? Organizational bystanders are folks who fail to act when their organization is in peril. Speak up. If you don't think it's a good idea, say so (Gerstein and Shaw 2008).

- When was the last time you took a vacation? One of the great benefits of working is getting vacation days. Whether you are an internal or external practitioner, take the opportunity to relax and reflect.

- Do you have a passport? This may seem trivial but according to the U.S. State Department (2012), only about 30 percent of

U.S. citizens have a passport. In 2011 about 12.5 million U.S. passports were issued, compared to 8.8 million in 2004. There are some distinct advantages of having a passport, including:

» travel opportunities for employees of a global company

» limitless travel options

» opportunity to experience local cultures

» great restaurants serve authentic meals in places like Little Italy, but the experience of visiting Italy lasts a lifetime.

- What is your technology prowess? Do you have a smartphone, but still rely on your paper calendar?

- Do you spend enough time with family and friends? Take time out from work and spend it with your family. Don't just do it on holidays; take time to appreciate the sacrifices your family makes for your success.

Appendix I:
An OD Action Research (AR) Checklist

Directions: Use these checklists to ensure that you are properly navigating the OD action research process. The aim is to achieve mutual understanding and collaboration, as well as increased insight and capabilities, as you move from step to step. Each checklist should be completed prior to moving to the next.

For each action statement appearing in the left had column, check the box for Yes, No, or N/A (not applicable) in the center column and write any appropriate notes in the right column.

Step 1: Entry

Key point: How you manage this phase will help you set the tone of your relationship with your client and create an environment for diagnostic and intervention work.

Did You:	Response			Notes
	Yes	No	N/A	
Make initial contact	☐	☐	☐	
Communicate who you are	☐	☐	☐	
Support the client in defining the issues, problems, and needs for change within the organization	☐	☐	☐	
Explore perspectives of the different stakeholders	☐	☐	☐	
Develop an understanding of the organization	☐	☐	☐	
Explore the capabilities and resources available to support the changes	☐	☐	☐	
Identify how the organization assesses its employees' competencies	☐	☐	☐	
Explore the client's readiness to move on the issues stated	☐	☐	☐	
Identify the appropriate decision maker, and who will be involved	☐	☐	☐	
Build a trusting relationship	☐	☐	☐	

Step 2: Feedback (A Two-Way Process)

Key point: Contracting is repetitive and continually renewable. As you employ the AR framework and gather data that broadens your and your client's understanding of the issues, you will need to revisit the contract. Remember to make a relationship contract and task contract.

Did You:	Response			Notes
	Yes	No	N/A	
Identify and confirm the relevant client groups for the intervention	☐	☐	☐	
Clarify and identify critical success factors and the real issues for the intervention	☐	☐	☐	
Agree to the scope (dates and budget) of the intervention	☐	☐	☐	
Agree on the internal liaison to administer the interventions	☐	☐	☐	
Link success factors into the organization's culture and processes	☐	☐	☐	
Clarify roles for the consultant and participating group	☐	☐	☐	
Sign the initial contract to facilitate the next step	☐	☐	☐	

Step 3: Assessment and Diagnosis

Key point: The quality of the diagnosis will affect how your clients plan the approach to change. If you handle this process well, you will pass important skills to the client organization on how to generate data for ongoing decision making.

Did You:	Response			Notes
	Yes	No	N/A	
Work out what type of data will help move the intervention forward	☐	☐	☐	
Work out required logistics and timelines	☐	☐	☐	
Design the most suitable methods, given the culture of the organization	☐	☐	☐	
Decide who to involve in analyzing and making sense of the data	☐	☐	☐	
Decide who should be involved in the feedback	☐	☐	☐	
Collect data to find different intervention options	☐	☐	☐	
Make a diagnosis, in order to recommend appropriate interventions	☐	☐	☐	
Revisit the contract and make revisions	☐	☐	☐	

Step 4: Feedback (A Two-Way Process)

Key point: This provides an opportunity for the entire organization to become involved in the change process, learn about how different units of the organization affect each other, and participate in identifying and selecting appropriate change interventions.

Did You:	Response			Notes
	Yes	No	N/A	
Report back what was found based on an analysis of the data	☐	☐	☐	
Make sure that everyone who contributed information has an opportunity to learn about the findings (provided there is no apparent breach of anyone's confidentiality)	☐	☐	☐	
Initiate the feedback with the executive client and his team, and cascade down through the organization to reach all who have participated	☐	☐	☐	

Step 5: Planning Change

Key point: Plan and ensure a participative decision-making process for the intervention.

Did You:	Response			Notes
	Yes	No	N/A	
Extract and summarize recommendations from the assessment and feedback	☐	☐	☐	
Consider alternative actions	☐	☐	☐	
Focus the intervention on activities that have the most leverage to effect positive change in the organization	☐	☐	☐	
Develop an implementation plan that is based on the data and logically organized, results-oriented, measurable, and rewarded				

Step 6: Intervention

Key point: It is important to follow the action plan, but also remain flexible enough to modify the process as the organization changes and as new information becomes available.

Did You:	Response			Notes
	Yes	No	N/A	
Carry out the action plan	☐	☐	☐	
Make sure that there are a few early, highly visible successes to increase support for the change effort	☐	☐	☐	
Determine a timing for the implementation that is appropriate (avoid peak work periods in the organization)	☐	☐	☐	

Step 7: Evaluation

Key point: Successful OD must make meaningful changes in the performance and efficiency of the organization.

Did You:	Response			Notes
	Yes	No	N/A	
Confirm this success through an evaluation, and identify needs for new or continuing OD activities	☐	☐	☐	
Evaluate how successfully the action plan was implemented	☐	☐	☐	
Assess how well the change effort contributed to the realization of the expectations of the leaders who initiated the change process	☐	☐	☐	
Improve the OD process to help make future interventions more successful	☐	☐	☐	

Step 8: Adoption

Key point: The new way of doing things should be instilled into the organization's culture.

Did You:	Response			Notes
	Yes	No	N/A	
Implement processes to ensure that the new way of doing things remains an ongoing activity in the organization	☐	☐	☐	
Obtain commitments for action	☐	☐	☐	

Step 9: Separation

Key point: Practitioners need to know how to be ready to change their strategy when necessary. An organization is dynamic, and may change while you are assessing it. You may need to move back and repeat previous steps in light of new information. And, as learning is really an iterative, not a sequential process, we must be prepared to re-enter this process when and where appropriate.

Did You:	Response			Notes
	Yes	No	N/A	
Recognize when it was more productive for you to undertake other activities—when continued consultation is counterproductive	☐	☐	☐	
Monitor the change to plan for future change activities	☐	☐	☐	

Sources: French and Bell (1995); Rothwell and Sullivan (2005).

Appendix II:
The International Organization Development Code of Ethics (22nd Revision)

○────────────────────●

The purpose of the Organization Development Institute in developing an International OD Code of Ethics is threefold: to increase professional and ethical consciousness among OD professionals and their sense of ethical responsibility, to guide OD professionals in making more informed ethical choices, and to help the OD profession function at the fullness of its potential.

We recognize that for us to exist as a profession, a substantial consensus is necessary among the members of our profession about what we profess, particularly our values and ethics. This statement represents a step toward such a consensus.

Recognizing that a profession cannot be a profession unless it has a code of ethics, we decided in 1980 to write an International Code of Ethics, not just for the OD Institute, but for the entire OD field. Working with people from all over the world, Bill Gellermann, RODC, put together an International Code of Ethics. The first draft was written by

Donald Cole, RODC, in the spring of 1981. It was published in the OD Institute's monthly newsletter, *Organizations and Change*, and a revised version was published in the 1982 edition of *The International Registry of OD Professionals*.

In the fall of 1981 Gellerman accepted the chairmanship of a committee to write a code of ethics for the global OD profession. With assistance from the OD Institute and others, he actively investigates all objections to each new version of the ethics code and then makes revisions to resolve those objections. The International OD Code of Ethics has been published in Polish, German, Spanish, Russian, and Hungarian. Contributions have come from Belgium, Canada, France, Germany, Great Britain, Hungary, India, Israel, Japan, the Netherlands, Norway, Poland, Saudi Arabia, South Africa, Spain, the United States, and Yugoslavia.

Most of the world's major OD organizations have agreed that it would be useful to have a commonly accepted international code of ethics for all OD professionals. Gellermann was awarded the OD Institute's Outstanding OD Consultant of the Year Award in 1984 for his work.

The following is the current version of the OD Code of Ethics.

Values of OD Professionals

As an OD professional, I acknowledge the fundamental importance of the following values both for myself and my profession:

1. quality of life—people being satisfied with their whole life experience

2. health, human potential, empowerment, growth and excellence—people being healthy, aware of the fullness of their potential, recognizing their power to bring that potential into being, growing into it, living it, and, generally, doing the best they can with it, individually and collectively

3. freedom and responsibility—people being free and responsible in choosing how they will live their lives

4. justice—people living lives whose results are fair and right for everyone

5. dignity, integrity, worth and fundamental rights of individuals, organizations, communities, societies, and other human systems

6. all-win attitudes and cooperation—people caring about one another and about working together to achieve results that work for everyone, individually and collectively

7. authenticity and openness in relationships

8. effectiveness, efficiency, and alignment—people achieving the maximum of desired results, at minimum cost, in ways that coordinate their individual energies and purposes with those of the system-as-a-whole, the subsystems of which they are parts, and the larger system of which their system is a part

9. holistic, systemic view, and stakeholder orientation—understanding human behavior from the perspective of whole system(s) that influence and are influenced by that behavior; recognizing the interests that different people have in the system's results and valuing those interests fairly and justly

10. wide participation in system affairs, confrontation of issues leading to effective problem solving, and democratic decision making.

Ethical Guidelines for OD Professionals

As an OD professional, I commit myself to supporting and acting in accordance with the following ethical guidelines:

I. Responsibility to Self

    A. Act with integrity; be authentic and true to myself.

    B. Strive continually for self-knowledge and personal growth.

    C. Recognize my personal needs and desires and, when they

conflict with other responsibilities, seek all-win resolutions of those conflicts.

  D. Assert my own economic and financial interests in ways that are fair and equitable to me as well as to my clients and their stakeholders.

II. Responsibility for Professional Development and Competence

  A. Accept responsibility for the consequences of my acts and make reasonable efforts to ensure that my services are properly used; terminate my services if they are not properly used and do what I can to see that any abuses are corrected.

  B. Strive to achieve and maintain a professional level of competence for both myself and my profession by developing the full range of my own competence and by establishing collegial and cooperative relations with other OD professionals.

  C. Recognize my own personal needs and desires and deal with them responsibly in the performance of my professional roles.

  D. Practice within the limits of my competence, culture, and experience in providing services and using techniques.

  E. Practice in cultures different from my own only with consultation from people native to or knowledgeable about those specific cultures.

III. Responsibility to Clients and Significant Others

  A. Serve the long-term well-being, interests, and development of the client system and all its stakeholders, even when the work being done has a short-term focus.

  B. Conduct any professional activity, program or relationship in ways that are honest, responsible, and appropriately open.

  C. Establish mutual agreement on a contract covering services and remuneration.

  D. Deal with conflicts constructively and avoid conflicts of interest as much as possible.

E. Define and protect the confidentiality of my client-professional relationships.

F. Make public statements of all kinds accurately, including promotion and advertising, and give service as advertised.

IV. Responsibility to the Profession

  A. Contribute to continuing professional development for myself, other practitioners, and the profession.

  B. Promote the sharing of OD knowledge and skill.

  C. Work with other OD professionals in ways that exemplary what our profession says we stand for.

  D. Work actively for ethical practice by individuals and organizations engaged in OD activities and, in case of questionable practice, use appropriate channels for dealing with it.

  E. Act in ways that bring credit to the OD profession and with due regard for colleagues in other professions.

V. Social Responsibility

  A. Act with sensitivity to the fact that my recommendations and actions may alter the lives and well-being of people within my client systems and the larger systems of which they are subsystems.

  B. Act with awareness of the cultural filters which affect my view of the world, respect cultures different from my own, and be sensitive to cross-cultural and multi-cultural differences and their implications.

  C. Promote justice and serve the wellbeing of all life on Earth

  D. Recognize that accepting this statement as a guide for my behavior involves holding myself to a standard that may be more exacting than the laws of any countries in which I practice, the guidelines of any professional associations to which I belong, or the expectations of any of my clients.

Notes: The process that produced this statement (currently in its 22nd version) was begun in 1981. It has been supported by most OD oriented professional organizations, associations, and networks in the United States of America. It was also supported unanimously by the participants at the 1984 OD World Congress in Southampton, England. To date, more than 200 people from more than 15 countries have participated in the process (the endorsements are of the process and not the statement.) The process included drafting a version, sending it out with a request for comments and suggestions, redrafting based on the responses, sending it out again, and so on. Our aim has been to use the process to establish a substantial consensus including acknowledgment of the differences among us.

By providing a common reference for OD professionals throughout the world, we seek to enhance our sense of identity as a global professional community. Because this statement was initially developed within the United States, adapting it to other cultures is necessary.

Bibliography

Abrams, N.D. 2011. "Temperament and Personality Assessments: Tools for Mediators?" *Dispute Resolution Journal* 66(4): 56-74.

Adams, J.D. 2003. "Successful Change: Paying Attention to the Intangibles." *OD Practitioner* 35(4): 3-7.

Aiken, M., M. Vanjani, and J. Krosp. 1995. "Group Decision Support Systems." *Review of Business* 16(3): 38.

Anderson, D.L. (2013). *Organization Development: The Process of Leading Organizational Change*, 2nd ed. Thousand Oaks, CA: SAGE.

Appelbaum, S.H., A. Chahrazad, and B.T. Shapiro. 1999. "The Self-Directed Team." *Team Performance Management* 5(2): 60. doi: 10.1108/13527599910268940.

"Appreciative Inquiry: Solving Problems by Looking at What's Going Right." *Mind Tools*. www.mindtools.com/pages/article/newTMC_85.htm.

Arneson, J., W.J. Rothwell, and J. Naughton. 2013. *ASTD Competency Study: The Training & Development Profession Redefined*. Alexandria, VA: ASTD Press.

Aronson, D. 1992. "Overview of Systems Thinking." *The Thinking Page*. www .thinking.net/Systems_Thinking/Intro_to_ST/intro_to_st.html.

Bartel-Radic, A., and N. Lesca. 2011. "Do Intercultural Teams Need Requisite Variety to be Effective?" *Management International* 15(3): 89-104.

Beckham, R. 1998. "Self-Directed Work Teams: The Wave of the Future?" *Hospital Materiel Management Quarterly* 20(1): 48-60.

Beckhard, R. 1969. *Organization Development: Strategies and Models*. Reading, MA: Addison-Wesley.

Beer, M., and Spector, B. 1993. "Organizational Diagnosis: Its Role in Organizational Learning." *Journal of Counseling and Development* 71(6): 642-650.

Block, P. 2011. *Flawless Consulting: A Guide to Getting Your Expertise Used*. 3rd ed. San Francisco: Pfeiffer.

Brown, S.L., and K.M. Eisenhardt. 1997. "The Art of Continuous Change: Linking Complexity Theory and Time-Paced Evolution in Relentlessly Shifting Organizations." *Administrative Science Quarterly* 42(1): 1-34.

Buchanan, D., L. Fitzgerald, D. Ketley, R. Gollop, J.L. Jones, S.S. Lamont, A. Neath, and E. Whitby. 2005. "No Going Back: A Review of the Literature on Sustaining Organizational Change." *International Journal of Management Reviews* 7:189-205. doi:10.1111/j.1468-2370.2005.00111.x.

Bunker, B.B., B.T. Alban, and R.J. Lewicki. 2004. "Ideas in Currency and OD Practice: Has the Well Gone Dry?" *The Journal of Applied Behavioral Science* 40:403-422. doi:10.1177/0021886304270372.

Burke, W.W. 2013. *Organization Change: Theory and Practice*, 4th ed. Thousand Oaks, CA: Sage.

Burke, W.W. 1994. *Organization Development: A Process of Learning and Changing*. 2nd ed. Reading, MA: Addison-Wesley.

Burke, W.W. 1982. *Organization Development: Principles and Practices*. Boston: Little, Brown.

Burke, W.W., and Litwin, G. H. 1992. "A Causal Model of Organizational Performance and Change." *Journal of Management* 18(3): 523-545.

Burnes, B. 2005. "Complexity Theories and Organizational Change." *International Journal of Management Reviews* 7:73-90. doi: 10.1111/j.1468-2370.2005.00107.x.

Burnes, B. 2004. "Kurt Lewin and Complexity Theories: Back to the Future?" *Journal of Change Management* 4(4): 309-325.

Bushe, G.R., and R.J. Marshak. 2014. *Dialogic Organization Development*. San Francisco: Wiley-Pfeiffer, 193-211.

Bushe, G.R., and R.J. Marshak. 2009. "Revisioning Organization Development: Diagnostic and Dialogic Premises and Patterns of Practice." *The Journal of Applied Behavioral Science* 45:348-368. doi:10.1177/0021886309335070.

Cady, S.H., J. Auger, and M. Foxon. 2010. "Situational Evaluation." In *Practicing Organization Development: A Guide for Leading Change*, 3rd ed., edited by W.J. Rothwell, J.M. Stavros, R.L. Sullivan, and A. Sullivan, 269-286. San Francisco: Pfeiffer.

Cady, S.H., and K.D. Dannemiller. 2005. "Whole System Transformation: The Five Truths of Change." In *Practicing Organization Development: A Guide for Consultants*, edited by W.J. Rothwell and R. Sullivan, 440-445. San Francisco: John C. Wiley & Sons.

Caya, O., M. Mortensen, and A. Pinsonneault. 2013. "Virtual Teams Demystified: An Integrative Framework for Understanding Virtual Teams." *International Journal of e-Collaboration* 9(2): 1-33.

Chapman, J.A. 2002. "A Framework for Transformational Change in Organizations." *Leadership & Organization Development Journal* 23(1):16-25.

Chartered Institute of Personnel and Development. 2013. "Coaching and Mentoring: Resource Summary." www.cipd.co.uk/hr-resources/factsheets/coaching-mentoring.aspx.

Cheung-Judge, M., and L. Holbeche. 2011. *Organization Development: A Practitioner's Guide for OD and HR*. London: Kogan Page.

Church, A.H., J. Waclawski, and W.W. Burke. 1996. "OD Practitioners as Facilitators of Change." Group & Organization Management 21:22-66. doi:10.1177/1059601196211003.

Chytas, P., M. Glykas, and G. Valiris. 2011. "A Proactive Balanced Scorecard." *International Journal of Information Management* 31(5): 460-468.

Cooperrider, D. L., and Whitney, D. 2005. *Appreciative Inquiry: A Positive Revolution in Change*. San Francisco: Berrett Koehler.

Cummings, T.G., and C.G. Worley. 2014. *Organization Development and Change*. Boston: Cengage Learning.

Douglas, C., J.S. Martin, and R.H. Krapels. 2006. "Communication in the Transition to Self-Directed Work Teams." *Journal of Business Communication* 43(4): 295-321. doi: 10.1177/002194360291704.

Doyle, R.J. 1992. "Caution: Self-Directed Work Team." *HR Magazine* 37:6.

Dubois, D.D., and W. J. Rothwell. 2004. *Competency-Based Human Resource Management*. Palo Alto, CA: Davies-Black Publishing.

Eason, K.E. 2008. "Sociotechnical Systems Theory in the 21st Century: Another Half-Filled Glass?" *In Sense in Social Science: A Collection of Essays in Honour of Dr. Lisl Klein*, edited by D. Graves and J. Marks, 123-134. Broughton-in-Furness, Cumbria, UK: Desmond Graves.

Edwards, M.R., and A.J. Ewen. 1996. *360° Feedback: The Powerful New Model for Employee Assessment & Performance Improvement*. New York: AMACOM American Management Association.

Eoyang, G.H. 2010. "Human Systems Dynamics: Competencies for a New Organizational Practice." In *Practicing Organization Development: A Guide for Leading Change*, 3rd ed., edited by W.J. Rothwell, J.M. Stavros, R.L. Sullivan, and A. Sullivan, 465-475. San Francisco: Pfeiffer.

Everything DiSC. 2010. "DiSC Overview." www.discprofile.com/what-is-disc /overview.

Falletta, S.A. 2005. *Organization Diagnostic Models: A Review and Synthesis*. A whitepaper. *Leadersphere*.

Few, S. 2006. *Information Dashboard Design: The Effective Visual Communication of Data*. Sebastopol, CA: O'Reilly Media.

Few, S. 2004. "Dashboard Confusion." *Intelligent Enterprise* 7(4): 14-15.

Filev, A. 2008. "Top-down and Bottom-up Project Management: Leveraging the Advantages of the Two Approaches." Project Management 2.0. February 8, www.wrike.com/projectmanagement/02/07/2008/Top-down-and-Bottom-up -Project-Management-Leveraging-the-Advantages-of-the-Two-Approaches.

Folkman, J.R. 2006. *The Power of Feedback: 35 Principles for Turning Feedback From Others Into Personal and Professional Change*. Hoboken, NJ: John C. Wiley & Sons.

Fox, W.M. 1995. "Sociotechnical System Principles and Guidelines: Past and Present." *Journal of Applied Behavioral Science* 31(1): 91-105. doi:10.1177/002188639511009.

French, W.L., and C.H. Bell Jr. 1999. *Organization Development: Behavioral Science Interventions for Organization Improvement*, 6th ed. Upper Saddle River, NJ: Prentice-Hall.

Gallagher, R.A. 2012. "About T-Groups: Congretional Development." www.congregationaldevelopment.com/storage/About%20T-groups.pdf.

Gerstein, M.S., and R.B. Shaw. 2008. "Organizational Bystanders." *People and Strategy* 31(1): 47-54.

Getnick, N. 2013. "In Wake of Corporate Scandals, a Reminder That Integrity Is Good Business." *International Business Times*, September 4. www.ibtimes .com/fighting-words/wake-corporate-scandals-reminder-integrity-good -business-1402617.

Ghosh, K., and S. Sahney. 2011. "Impact of Organizational Sociotechnical System on Managerial Retention." *Journal of Modeling in Management* 6(1): 33-39. doi:10.1108/17465661111112/194

Golden-Biddle, K., and L.Y. Team. 2013. "How to Change an Organization Without Blowing It Up." *MIT Sloan Management Review* 54(2): 35-41.

Grobman, G.M. 2005. "Complexity Theory: A New Way to Look at Organization Change." *Public Administration Quarterly* 29(3): 350-383.

Haavik, T.K. 2011. "On Components and Relations in Sociotechnical Systems." *Journal of Contingences and Crisis Management* 19(2). doi:10.111/j1468-5973.2011.00638.x.

Halverson, C.B. 2008. "Team Development." In *Effective Multicultural Teams: Theory and Practice*, edited by C.B. Halverson and S.A. Trimizi, 81-110. doi: 10.1007/978-1-4020-6957-4.

Hamilton, E.E. 1988. "The Facilitation of Organizational Change: An Empirical Study of Factors Predicting Change Agents' Effectiveness." *Journal of Applied Behavioral Science* 24:37-59. doi:10.1177/0021886388241006.

Hammer, M., and J. Champy. 1993. *Reengineering the Corporation: A Manifesto for Business*. New York: HarperCollins.

Harrison, M.I. 2005. *Diagnosing Organizations: Methods, Models, and Processes*. 3rd ed. Thousand Oaks, CA: Sage.

Hawkins, P., and N. Smith. 2013. *Coaching, Mentoring and Organizational Consultancy: Supervision, Skills And Development*. Berkshire, England: McGraw-Hill International.

Head, T.C., and P.F. Sorensen Jr. 2005. "The Evaluation of Organization Development Interventions: An Empirical Study." *Organization Development Journal* 23(1): 40-55.

Heylighen, E., and C. Joslyn. 1992. "What Is Systems Theory?" http://pespmc1.vub.ac.be/SYSTHEOR.html.

Holweg, M. 2007. "The Genealogy of Lean Production." *Journal of Operations Management* 25(2): 420-437.

Howard, A., and Associates. 1994. *Diagnosis for Organizational Change. Methods and Models*. New York: Guilford.

Jacobs, R.L. 2002. "Institutionalizing Organizational Change Through Cascade Training." *Journal of European Industrial Training* 26:177-182. doi:10.1108/03090590210422058.

Jarocki, T.L. 2011. *The Next Evolution: Enhancing and Unifying Project and Change Management*. San Francisco: Brown & Williams.

Járos, G.G. 1995. "The Organization as a Doublet." *Systems Practice* 8:69-83. doi:10.1007/BF02249177.

Kalra, N., and S. Gupta. 2014. "Succession Planning in SMEs: An Empirical Analysis." *International Journal of Research in Management and Social Science* 2(2): 124-133.

Kaner, S. 2014. *Facilitator's Guide to Participatory Decision-Making*. San Francisco: Jossey-Bass.

Kanter, R.M., B.A. Stein, and T.D. Jick. 1992. *The Challenge of Organizational Change: How Companies Experience It and Leaders Guide It*. New York: Free Press.

Kaplan, R.S., and D.P. Norton. 1996. "Using the Balanced Scorecard as a Strategic Management System." *Harvard Business Review* 74(1): 75-85.

Kaplan, R.S., and D.P. Norton. 1992. "The Balanced Scorecard: Measures That Drive Performance." *Harvard Business Review* 70(1): 71-79.

Katz, D., and R.L. Kahn. 1978. *The Social Psychology Of Organizations*. 2nd ed. New York: Wiley.

Kauffeld, S. 2006. "Self-Directed Work Groups and Team Competence." *Journal of Occupational and Organizational Psychology* 79(1): 21.

Kaynak, E., R.M. Fulmer, and J.B. Keys. 2013. *Executive Development and Organizational Learning for Global Business*. New York: Routledge.

Kezar, A. 2001. "Understanding and Facilitating Organizational Change in the 21st Century: Recent Research and Conceptualizations." Washington, DC: ASHE-ERIC Higher Education Reports. *Sloan Management Review*, 12, 51-65.

Kirkpatrick, D.L., and J.D. Kirkpatrick. 2006. *Evaluating Training Programs: The Four Levels*. 3rd ed. San Francisco: Barrett-Koehler.

Kotter, J.P. 2012. *Leading Change*. Boston, MA: Harvard Business Review Press.

Kotter, J.P. 1995. "Leading Change: Why Transformation Efforts Fail." *Harvard Business Review* 73(2): 59-67.

Krell, T.C. 1981. "The Marketing of Organization Development: Past, Present, and Future." *Journal of Applied Behavioral Science* 17:309-323. doi:10.1177/002188638101700304.

Kurpius, D.J., and D.R. Fuqua. 1993. "Fundamental Issues in Defining Consultation." *Journal of Counseling & Development* 71:598-600. doi:10.1002/j.1556-6676.1993.tb02248.x.

Lacey, M.Y. 1995. "Internal Consulting: Perspectives on the Process of Planned Change." *Journal of Organizational Change Management* 8(3): 75-84. doi:10.1108/09534819510090178.

Lai, A.V.H. 2014. "Organization Redesign and Leadership Legitimacy in Pluralistic Organizations: A Communicative Framework." PhD diss. University of St. Gallen.

Levitt, T. 1960. "Marketing Myopia." *Harvard Business Review* 38(4): 45-56.

Liker, J.K. 2004. *The Toyota Way: 14 Management Principles From the World's Greatest Manufacturer*. New York: McGraw-Hill.

Lippitt, G., and R. Lippitt. 1986. *The Consulting Process in Action*, 2nd ed. San Francisco: Jossey-Bass/Pfeiffer.

Livingston, R.E. 2006. "Evaluation and Termination Phase." In *The NTL Handbook of Organization Development and Change: Principles, Practices, and Perspectives*, edited by B.B. Jones and M. Brazzel, 231-245. San Francisco: Pfeiffer.

Ludema, J.D. 2000. "From Deficit Discourse to Vocabularies of Hope: The Power of Appreciation." In *Appreciative Inquiry: Rethinking Human Organization Toward a Positive Theory or Change*, edited by D. Cooperrider. Champaign, IL: Stipes Publishing.

Ludema, J.D., D.L. Cooperrider, and F.J. Barrett. 2001. "Appreciative Inquiry: The Power of the Unconditional Positive Question." In *The Handbook of Action Research*, edited by P. Reason and H. Bradbury. Thousand Oaks, CA: Sage.

Luft, J., and H. Ingham. 1955. *The Johari-Window: A Graphic Model for Interpersonal Relations*. Los Angeles: University of California Western Training Lab.

Lundberg, C.C. 2008. "Organization Development Diagnosis." In *Handbook of Organization Development*, edited by T.G. Cummings, 137-150. Thousand Oaks, CA: Sage.

Manz, C.C. 1992. "Self-Leading Work Teams: Moving Beyond Self-Management Myths." *Human Relations* 45(11): 1119. doi:10.177/001872679204501101.

Marshak, R. 2006. *Covert Processes at Work: Managing the Five Hidden Dimensions of Organizational Change*. San Francisco: Berrett-Koehler.

McLachlin, R.D. 1999. "Factors for Consulting Engagement Success." *Management Decision* 37:394-404. doi:10.1108/00251749910274162.

McLean, G.N. 2006. *Organization Development: Principles, Processes, Performance*. San Francisco: Berrett-Koehler.

McNamara, C. 2006. *Field Guide to Consulting and Organizational Development: A Collaborative and Systems Approach to Performance, Change, and Learning.* Minneapolis, MN: Authenticity Consulting, LLC.

Meyer, C. 1994. "How the Right Measures Help Teams Excel." *Harvard Business Review* 72(3): 95-103.

Mohr, A. 2013. "5 Most Publicized Ethics Violations by CEOs." *Investopedia.* January 30. www.investopedia.com/financial-edge/0113/5-most-publicized -ethics-violations-by-ceos.aspx.

Morrison, P. 1986. "Evaluation in OD: A Review and an Assessment." *Group & Organization Studies* 3:42-70. doi:10.1177/105960117800300106.

Mumford, E. 2000. "A Socio-Technical Approach to Systems Design." *Requirements Engineering* 5(2):125-133. doi:10.1007/PL00010345.

Muthusamy, S.K., J.V. Wheeler, and B.L. Simmons. 2005. "Self-Managing Work Teams: Enhancing Organizational Innovativeness." *Organization Development Journal* 23(3): 53-66.

Myers, I.B., L.K. Kirby, and K.D. Myers. 1993. *Introduction to Type*, 5th ed. Palo Alto, CA: Consulting Psychologists.

O'Brien, R. 1998. "An Overview of the Methodological Approach of Action Research." In *Theory and Practice of Action Research*, edited by R. Richardson, João Pessoa, Brazil. www.web.ca/robrien/papers/arfinal.html.

Peters, T.J., and R.H. Waterman. 1982. *In Search of Excellence: Lessons from America's Best-Run Companies.* New York: Harper and Row.

Pettigrew, A.M., R.W. Woodman, and K.S. Cameron. 2001. "Studying Organization Change and Development: Changes for Future Research." *Academy of Management Journal* 44(4): 697-713.

Phelps, J. 2005. "Ten Steps to Deploying Self-Directed Teams." *Cost Engineering* 47(6): 36.

Phillips, P.P., and J.J. Phillips. 2005. *Return on Investment (ROI) Basics.* Alexandria, VA: ASTD Press.

Piotrowski, C., and T.R. Armstrong. 2004. "The Research Literature in Organization Development: Recent Trends and Current Directions." *Organization Development Journal* 22(2): 48.

"Project Management." (n.d.). Wikipedia, last modified January 31, 2014, http://en.wikipedia.org/wiki/Project_management.

Pyzdek, T., and P. Keller. 2009. *The Six Sigma Handbook*, 3rd ed. New York: McGraw Hill.

Raab, N. 2013. "Working With the Client-Consultant Relationship: Why Every Step Is an Intervention." In *Handbook for Strategic HR: Best Practices in Organization Development From the OD Network*, edited by J. Vogelsang, M. Townsend, M. Minahan, D. Jamieson, J. Vogel, A. Viets, C. Royal, and L. Valek, 76-81. New York: AMACOM.

Rahschulte, T.J., W. Herrli, and D. Herrli. 2009. *The Most Important Aspect of Project Management Today: Determining Readiness for Change. PMI Global Congress 2009—North America. Proceedings.* Newtown Square, PA: Project Management Institute.

Reason, P., and K.L. McArdle. 2007. "Action Research and Organization Development." In *Handbook of Organization Development*, edited by T.G. Cummings, 123-137. Thousand Oaks, CA: Sage Publications.

Reason, P., and H. Bradbury. 2001. Preface. In *Handbook of Action Research: Participative Inquiry and Practice*, edited by P. Reason and H. Bradbury, xxiii-xxxi. London: Sage Publications.

Recklies, D. 2007. "The 7-S-Model." March 18. www.themanager.org /Models/7S%20Model.htm.

Rigopoulos, G., J. Psarras, and D.T. Askounis. 2008. "Web Support System for Group Collaborative Decisions." *Journal of Applied Sciences* 8(3): 407-419.

Roland, D.G. 2014. "Learning Organization and Human Motivation." www .apaessayformat.com/organizational-behaviour/learning-organization -human-motivation.htm.

Rothwell, W.J. 2005. *Effective Succession Planning: Ensuring Leadership Continuity and Building Talent From Within*, 3rd ed. New York: AMACOM.

Rothwell, W.J. 2010. *Effective Succession Planning*, 4th ed. New York: AMACOM.

Rothwell, W.J., and Chee, P. 2013. *Becoming an Effective Mentoring Leader: Proven Strategies for Building Excellence in Your Organization.* New York: McGraw-Hill.

Rothwell, W.J., and H.J. Sredl. 1992. *ASTD Reference Guide to Professional Human Resource Development Roles and Competencies*, Vol. 2, 2nd ed. Amherst, MA: HRD Press.

Rothwell, W.J., J.M. Stavros, R.L. Sullivan, and A. Sullivan. 2010. *Practicing Organization Development: A Guide for Leading Change.* 3rd ed. San Francisco: Pfeiffer.

Rothwell, W.J., and R. Sullivan. 2005. *Practicing Organization Development: A Guide for Consultants*, 2nd ed. San Francisco, CA: John C. Wiley & Sons.

Sarker, S., Lau, F., and Sahay, S. 2001. "Using an Adapted Grounded Theory Approach for Inductive Theory Building About Virtual Team Development." *Data Base* 32(1): 38-56.

Schein, E. 1999. *Process Consultation Revisited*. Boston: Addison Wesley.

Schein, E. 1992. *Organizational Culture and Leadership: A Dynamic View*. San Francisco: Jossey-Bass.

Scott, B. 2008. "Consulting on the Inside." In *ASTD Handbook for Workplace Learning Professionals*, edited by E. Biech, 671-689. Alexandria, VA: ASTD Press.

Scott, B., and B.K. Barnes. 2011. *Consulting on the Inside: A Practical Guide for Internal Consultants*. Alexandria, VA: ASTD Press.

Senge, P.M., A. Kleiner, C. Roberts, R.B. Ross, and B.J. Smith. 1994. *The Fifth Discipline Fieldbook*. New York: Currency Doubleday.

Shepard, K.O., and A.P. Raia. 1981. "The OD Training Challenge." *Training & Development Journal* 35(4): 90-96.

Strauch, B. 2010. "Can Cultural Differences Lead to Accidents? Team Cultural Difference and Sociotechnical Systems Operations." *Human Factors: The Journal of the Human Factors and Ergonomics Society* 52(246). doi: 10.1177/0018720810362238.

Sullivan, R.L., L.K. Fairburn, and W.J. Rothwell. 2002. "Whole Systems Transformation Conference: Fast Change for the 21st Century." In *Rewiring Organizations for the Networked Economy: Organizing, Managing, and Leading in the Information Age*, edited by S.M. Herman and F. Richard, 115-139. Hoboken, NJ: Wiley.

Sung, S.Y., and J.N. Choi. 2014. "Do Organizations Spend Wisely on Employees? Effects of Training and Development Investments on Learning and Innovation in Organizations." *Journal of Organizational Behavior* 35(3): 393-412.

Swanson, R.A. 1994. *Analysis for Improving Performance: Tools for Diagnosing Organizations and Documenting Workplace Expertise*. San Francisco: Barrette Koehler.

Tandon, R. 2013. "New Area in Johari Window." *Thinking* 3(2).

Teachers' PD INC. 2014. "Teachers' Professional Development for Inland California." www.csuchico.edu/teacher-grants/index.shtml.

Tichy, N.M., H.A. Hornstein, and J.N. Nisberg. 1977. "Organization Diagnosis and Intervention Strategies: Developing Emergent Pragmatic Theories of Change." In *Current Issue and Strategies in Organization Development*, edited by W.W. Burke, 361-383. New York: Human Sciences Press.

Tippins, N.T. 2002. "Organization Development and IT: Practicing OD in the Virtual World." In *Organization Development: A Data-Driven Approach to Organizational Change*, edited by J. Waclawski and A.H. Church, 245–265. San Francisco: Jossey-Bass.

Towers Watson. 2013. "Only One-Quarter of Employers Are Sustaining Gains From Change Management Initiatives, Towers Watson Survey Finds." www .towerswatson.com/en/Press/2013/08/Only-One-Quarter-of-Employers-Are -Sustaining-Gains-From-Change-Management.

Tuckman, B.W. 1965. "Developmental Sequence in Small Groups." *Psychological Bulletin* 63(6): 384-399. doi: 10.1037/h0022100.

U.S. State Department. 2012. http://travel.state.gov/passport/ppi/stats /stats_890.html.

Van de Ven, A., and D. Ferry. 1980. *Measuring and Assessing Organizations*. New York, NY: Wiley.

Van Eron, A.M., and W.W. Burke. 2010. "Closure: Freeing Up Energy to Move Forward." In *Practicing Organization Development: A Guide for Leading Change*, 3rd ed., edited by W.J. Rothwell, J.M. Stavros, R.L. Sullivan, and A. Sullivan, 287-297. San Francisco: Pfeiffer.

Varney, G. 1980. "Developing OD Competencies." *Training & Development Journal* 34(4): 30-35.

Von Bertalanffy, L. 1968. *General System Theory: Foundations, Developments, Applications*. New York: Braziller.

Waclawski, J., and A.H. Church. 2002. "Introduction and Overview of Organization Development as a Data-Driven Approach for Organizational Change." In *Organization Development: A Data-Driven Approach to Organizational Change*, edited by J. Waclawski and A.H. Church, 3-26. San Francisco: Jossey-Bass.

Waclawski, J., A.H. Church, and W.W. Burke. 1995. "Women and Men as Organizational Development Practitioners: An Analysis of Differences and Similarities." *Consulting Psychology Journal: Practice and Research* 47(2): 89-107.

Warrick, D.D. 2010. "Launch: Assessment, Action Planning, and Implementation." In *Practicing Organization Development: A Guide for Leading Change*, 3rd ed., edited by W.J. Rothwell, J.M. Stavros, R.L. Sullivan, and A. Sullivan, 234-268. San Francisco: Pfeiffer.

Waterman, R. Jr., T. Peters, and J.R. Phillips. 1980. "Structure is Not Organization." *Business Horizons* 23(3), 14-26.

Watkins, J.M., and J.M. Stavros. 2010. "Appreciative Inquiry." In *Practicing Organization Development: A Guide for Leading Change*, 2nd ed., edited by W. Rothwell and R. Sullivan. San Francisco: Pfeiffer.

Weick, K.E., and R.E. Quinn. 1999. "Organizational Change and Development." *Annual Review of Psychology* 50: 361–386.

Weiss, A. 2010. "Entry: Marketing and Positioning OD." In *Practicing Organization Development: A Guide for Leading Change*, 3rd ed., edited by W.J. Rothwell, J.M. Stavros, R.L. Sullivan, and A. Sullivan, 185-203. San Francisco: Pfeiffer.

Wheatley, H., R. Tannenbaun, P.Y. Griffin, and K. Quade, eds. 2003. "The Future." Chap. 5 in *Organization Development at Work: Conversations on the Values, Applications, and Future of OD*. San Francisco: Pfeiffer.

White, L.P., and K.C. Wooten. 1983. "Ethical Dilemmas in Various Stages of Organizational Development." *The Academy of Management Review* 8:690-697.

White, R.W. 1959. "Motivation Reconsidered: The Concept of Competence." *Psychological Review* 66:297-333. doi:10.1037/h0040934

Worley, C., and A. Feyerherm. 2003. "Reflections on the Future of Organization Development." *Journal of Applied Behavioral Science* 39:97-115. doi:10.1177/0021886303039001005

Worley, C., and G. Varney. 1998, Winter. "A Search for a Common Body of Knowledge for Master's Level Organization Development and Change Programs: An Invitation to Join the Discussion." *Academy of Management ODC Newsletter*, 1-3.

Worley, C.G., W.J. Rothwell, and R.L. Sullivan. 2010. "Competencies of OD Practitioners." In *Practicing Organization Development: A Guide for Leading Change*, 3rd ed., edited by W.J. Rothwell, J.M. Stavros, R.L. Sullivan, and A. Sullivan, 107-135. San Francisco: Pfeiffer.

Worren, N.A.M., K. Ruddle, and K. Moore. 1999. "From Organizational Development to Change Management: The Emergence of a New Profession." *The Journal of Applied Behavioral Science* 35:273-286. doi:10.1177/0021886399353002.

Yeatts, D.E., and C. Hyten, eds. 1998. "Roles of Self-Managed Teams." Chap. 25 in *High-Performing Self-Managed Work Teams: A Comparison Theory to Practice*. Thousand Oaks, CA: Sage.

Zakarian, A., and A. Kusiak. 1999. "Forming Teams: An Analytical Approach." *IIE Transactions* 31(1): 85-97. doi: 10.1080/07408179908969808.

Zimmerli, W.C., K. Richter, and M. Holzinger, eds. 2007. *Corporate Ethics and Corporate Governance*. New York: Springer.

Index

C

About the Authors

○————————●

William J. Rothwell, PhD, SPHR, CPLP Fellow, is professor of learning and performance in the workforce education and development program, department of learning and performance systems, at the Pennsylvania State University, University Park campus. In that capacity, he heads up a top-ranked graduate program in learning and performance. He has authored, co-authored, edited, or co-edited 300 books, book chapters, and articles—including more than 70 books. He is also president of his own consulting firm, Rothwell & Associates.

Before arriving at Penn State in 1993, he had 20 years of work experience as a training director in government and in business. He has also worked as a consultant for more than 40 multinational corporations—including Motorola, General Motors, Ford, and many others. In 2012, he was honored with ASTD's Distinguished Contribution to Workplace Learning and Performance Award, and in 2013 he was again honored by ASTD by being appointed a Certified Professional in Learning and Performance (CPLP) Fellow. His recent books include *Creating Engaged Employees: It's Worth the Investment*, *The Leader's Daily Role in Talent Management: Maximizing Results, Engagement and Retention*, *Optimizing Talent in the Federal Workforce*, *Performance Consulting*, *ASTD Competency*

Study: The Training and Development Profession Redefined, Becoming an Effective Mentoring Leader, Talent Management: An Action-Oriented Step-by-Step Approach, the edited three-volume *Encyclopedia of Human Resource Management, Lean But Agile: Rethink Workforce Planning and Gain a True Competitive Advantage*, and *Invaluable Knowledge*. He can be reached by email at wjr9@psu.edu.

Cavil S. Anderson earned a master's degree in education management, a bachelor's in teaching, and two international scholarships in education management. She is working toward a PhD in workforce education and development at the Pennsylvania State University. Her most recent research interest is the influence of organizational structure on learning in the workplace. Anderson is owner and director of the Center for Organization and Human Development (COHD). She has also directed various school-based, community-funded organization development and change interventions, including the program development unit at the Management of Schools Training Program, where she contributed to the development of a national school governance and ethics framework. She was awarded an international scholarship to the Netherlands for outstanding performance. Another career highlight was the acknowledgment of the Kathorus Projects with Premier Status that earned Anderson a second scholarship to the University of Connecticut. As project manager, Anderson led a collaborative intervention and developed a quality assurance framework and benchmarked operations in the center for course design and development at the University of South Africa. She also served as training and development coordinator at Kutztown University in Pennsylvania.

Cynthia M. Corn is a dual-PhD candidate in workforce education and comparative and international education at the Pennsylvania State University. She has more than 20 years of workforce education and consulting experience in positions of progressive responsibility that join international project and program management, international global governance, and sustainable development. With expertise in indigenous knowledge and transition cultures, she is dedicated to Native American cultural revitalization, economic development, justice, and peace building.

Catherine Haynes is a dual-PhD candidate in workforce education and comparative and international education at the Pennsylvania State University. Her research interests are in workforce education and tourism and hospitality education. She also holds an MS from Penn State, where her master's thesis was about the relationship between newly promoted supervisors and former co-workers. She teaches courses on human resources as an adjunct with the college of health and human development. Haynes is also a Fulbright-Hays Scholar, with educational experiences in Tanzania, Africa, and served with the U.S. Army for 22 years. Her main responsibilities were in all aspects of human resource management, training and development, and equal employment opportunity (EEO). Haynes is actively involved in the Workforce Education Society for Peer Mentoring (WSPM), the International Education Students Association (IESA), and the National Society of Minorities in Hospitality (NSMH).

Cho Hyun Park has a PhD in workforce education and development with an emphasis in human resource development and organization development at the Pennsylvania State University. She earned her master's degree in work and human resource education at the University of Minnesota-Twin Cities. She currently works for Samsung SDS as a principal HRD consultant. She also worked for Samsung Electronics as a human resource development professional for eight years, leading technology education for the company's semiconductor engineers and developing various technology education programs. In addition, Park has experience in online and blended learning and was involved in the proliferation of knowledge management within the company.

Aileen G. Zaballero, MS, CPLP, is a senior partner for R&A and a dual-title PhD candidate in workforce education and development and comparative international education, with an emphasis on organization development at the Pennsylvania State University. She has been a certified professional in learning and performance (CPLP) through ASTD since 2009. Her research focuses on the human factors and group processes that influence the competitive performance of businesses. Her recent publications include chapters in *Performance Consulting*, *Optimizing Talent in the Federal Workforce*, *The Competency Toolkit*, 2nd ed., *Encyclopedia of Human Resource Management*, vol. 2, and *Handbook of Research on Workforce Diversity in a Global Society*.